FROM AKHENATEN TO MOSES

FROM AKHENATEN TO MOSES

ANCIENT EGYPT AND RELIGIOUS CHANGE

JAN ASSMANN

The American University in Cairo Press
Cairo New York

This paperback edition published in 2016 by
The American University in Cairo Press
113 Sharia Kasr el Aini, Cairo, Egypt
420 Fifth Avenue, New York, NY 10018
www.aucpress.com

Exclusive distribution outside Egypt and North America by I.B.Tauris & Co Ltd., 6 Salem Road,
London, W2 4BU

Dar el Kutub No. 14304/15
ISBN 978 977 416 749 2

Dar el Kutub Cataloging-in-Publication Data

Assmann, Jan
    From Akhenaten to Moses: Ancient Egypt and Religious Change/Jan Assmann.—Cairo:
  The American University in Cairo Press, 2016
    p.   cm.
    ISBN: 978 977 416 749 2
    1. Moses (biblical leader)
    2. Akhenaton—king of Egypt
    3. Egypt—kings and rulers
    932

1 2 3 4 5   20 19 18 17 16

Designed by Adam el-Sehemy
Printed in Egypt

To Fayza Haikal and Salima Ikram
with friendship, gratitude, and admiration

CONTENTS

PREFACE

Five of the seven chapters of this book (1, 3, 4, 6, 7) are based on lectures delivered at the American University in Cairo in November 2012. I am grateful to my colleagues Fayza Haikal and Salima Ikram for the invitation and for all they did in order to make my stay in Cairo as agreeable as possible. Chapter 2 has evolved out of papers given at the universities of St Andrews, Tallinn, and Prague, and a first version of chapter 5 was presented at Boston University. All chapters profited enormously from the discussions at the various places of their first presentation in the course of the year 2012. I am also indebted to Fayza and Salima for correcting my English and suggesting modifications and clarifications where my formulations seemed all too dense or misleading. The red thread that runs through these chapters, and which will be explained in more detail in the introduction, is the topic of change in religion, beginning with ancient Egypt and ending with a dynamism that is as active in modern times as it was in antiquity.

INTRODUCTION

Akhenaten and Moses—two names that stand for the abolition of polytheism and the introduction of monotheism, a turn not only in religion but in the general intellectual orientation of humanity that changed the ancient world and brought about the world in which we are still living. All seven chapters of this book deal with this fundamental transformation. Their common subject is the question of change in the religions of Egypt and Israel and the search for the aspects and agents of religious transformation that affected not only the respective religions but the world in general. That this transformation was not so radical as is commonly thought, however, is shown in chapter 6, which deals with the European eighteenth century and its image of the Egyptian mysteries and shows that a repressed Egyptian polytheism continued in western thought as an undercurrent, gaining particular strength at the end of the eighteenth century.

The first chapter, "Structure and Change in Ancient Egyptian Religion," focuses on ancient Egyptian religion, seeking the specific traits of Egyptian religion in the frame of a general definition of religion. Religion is defined as containing at least three aspects or dimensions that must be realized in a specific way in any given religion in order to deserve the title 'religion': cult, theology, and a normative orientation concerning the guidance of life or moral conduct. There is no religion without any form of cult, there is no cult without any ideas of the divine it is serving and addressing, and there is no religion without impact on the way of life of its believers. In all three dimensions, ancient Egypt shows an outstanding and highly original profile. Whereas in the cultic dimension, there is an enormous amount of stability and continuity, fundamental and far-reaching changes may be observed in the fields of theology and lifestyle.

1

The implicit 'cosmogonic monotheism' typical of ancient Egypt, deriving everything that exists (including the gods) from one single divine source, the sun god, is made explicit in two ways: in a radically exclusivist form by the revolution of Akhenaten, and in an inclusivist form with the rise of the theological discourse that eventually arrived at the idea that all gods are One. This monistic theology of All-Oneness lives on as a countercurrent to western monotheism in the Hermetic and Neoplatonic traditions until today.

In the same way that chapter 1 is dedicated to ancient Egypt, chapter 2, "Myth and History of the Exodus: Triumph and Trauma," concentrates on ancient Israel and its foundational myth: the story of the Exodus from Egypt. The Biblical book of Exodus and the myth behind it are the narrative version of the great transformation that the turn from polytheism to Biblical monotheism meant for the ancient world. The interest of the story, in which ancient Egypt plays such an important and sinister role, lies not in what really happened but in how, by whom, when, in what form, and for what purpose it was told in the course of millennia.

The transformation from polytheism to monotheism with the Christianization and Islamization of the ancient world is mostly interpreted in terms of cultural evolution by historians of religion. Chapter 3, "From Polytheism to Monotheism: Evolution or Revolution?" confronts this concept with the idea of religious revolution. Evolution is a concept that (in spite of the antagonism between evolutionism and Christian creationism) is in itself strongly related to Christian thought. Religious evolutionism is born of a Christian perspective that gives the new precedence over the old. A more complete picture is gained if we complement evolution with revolution. In the turn from polytheism to monotheism, both dynamics are involved. This can be shown with regard to the Hebrew Bible in the coexistence of two seemingly contradictory trends: the covenant theology of loyalty, presupposing the existence of other gods but requiring exclusive faithfulness to Yahweh alone, and the true monotheistic universalism of Deutero-Isaiah, for whom there are no other gods. In Egypt, also, we meet with both dynamics. There is an unmistakable evolution of theological ideas, leading from the idea of a theology of creation and primacy (the creator acting as chief of the pantheon) to a theology of manifestation (the hidden God manifesting himself in the divine world), interrupted in the middle of the fourteenth century BCE by King Akhenaten's overthrowing of traditional religion and installation of the monotheistic cult of the Aten, a clear irruption of revolutionary monotheism.

The monotheist revolution of Akhenaten and the founding of Israelite monotheism by Moses have often been brought together, most famously by Sigmund Freud in his last book, *Moses and Monotheism*. Chapter 4, "Moses and Akhenaten: Memory and History," investigates the historical and mnemohistorical foundations of this problematic rapprochement. Akhenaten is a figure exclusively of history who was denied any tradition and memory in ancient Egyptian culture, having been subjected to a complete *damnatio memoriae*. Moses, on the other hand, is a figure exclusively of memory, accruing an immense importance as the founding father of monotheism in the Jewish, Christian, and Islamic traditions, of whose historical existence, however, not the least traces have been found. It is, therefore, small wonder that the two figures, complementing each other in such a perfect way, have often been brought together. There is, however, even a late Egyptian tradition identifying Akhenaten (called Osarseph) with Moses: Manetho's legend of the lepers, whose reference to the Amarna experience is corroborated by a passage in Diodorus on the pyramids. These and other sources show that there was a strong tradition in Egyptian cultural memory about three great catastrophes and times of suffering in the past and their triumphant overcoming, the Amarna experience being one of them. These traditions concerning Egyptian suffering and final triumph show striking parallels to the Biblical story of the Exodus that point to the fact that the Late Egyptian tradition (ca. 600 BCE onward) about Akhenaten-Osarseph and the Biblical tradition about Moses and the Exodus did not arise completely independently of each other.

The most comprehensive and influential theory of spiritual and intellectual change in the ancient world is the theory of the "Axial Age," which is dealt with in chapter 5, "Ancient Egypt and the Theory of the Axial Age." The great transformation that changed the ancient world and brought about the religious and intellectual foundations of the world in which we are still living started not in Egypt but in Palestine, with the rise of Judaism and Christianity. Since the late eighteenth century this event has been seen in the context of similar innovations and transformations that occurred in different civilizations—China, India, Persia, Israel, and Greece—at about the same time, around 500 BCE, the "Axial Age" (Karl Jaspers). Why did Egypt, unlike Israel, remain outside this spiritual revolution? This chapter focuses on the question of cultural memory and its media, and identifies canonization and exegesis as the decisive agents of change that created new means of relating to the past and thereby shaping the future.

However radically the world was changed by its Christianization in late antiquity and the extinction of the pagan cults, an undercurrent of Egyptian cosmotheism continued to haunt the west. Chapter 6, "Egyptian Mysteries and Secret Societies in the Age of Enlightenment," deals with European "Egyptomania" and its apex in the late eighteenth century. From the Renaissance onward, ancient Egypt came to be seen, on the basis of Greek, Latin, Hebrew, and Arabic texts, as a "dual culture," split into a popular and polytheistic culture and a secret and mono- or pantheistic one. This image was embraced by the secret societies of the eighteenth century as a model and mirror of their own situation and intellectual mission, imagining themselves as the true heirs of the ancient Egyptian priests. What brought about this identification with ancient Egypt was mainly the political interpretation of the ancient, especially Egyptian, mysteries. They were thought to secretly preserve and transmit the true ("natural") religion under the conditions of a state, based on a cult of fictitious deities that were believed to protect the law and to represent national power and identity. This theory had an enormous appeal to the Freemasons, Rosicrucians, and Illuminati, and found expression also in works of music (Mozart's *The Magic Flute*), literature (Schiller's "The Veiled Image at Sais" and many other poems and novels of initiation), and philosophy (C.L. Reinhold's *The Hebrew Mysteries*).

The last chapter, "Total Religion: Politics, Monotheism, and Violence," addresses the most immediate and disquieting aspect of religious change: the use of violence. Where does religious violence (violence committed in the name of God) come from? Its roots lie obviously in the polarizing power typical of monotheistic religions, dividing people into Jews and Gentiles, believers and non-believers, orthodox and heretics, and so on. The question is, what dynamism turns distinction into polarization, and polarization into mutual enmity, hatred, and violent conflict? The answer proposed here is based on Carl Schmitt's theory of political totalization. Under the conditions of *Ernstfall* (case of emergency, i.e., war), people associate and dissociate in terms of friend and foe and are ready to annihilate each other with physical violence. Schmitt uses this dynamic as an argument for the hegemony of the political over all other spheres of culture, such as law, economy, science, art, morality, and religion, and pleads for the total state.

This theory may be applied to religion, if there is something like a religious *Ernstfall* that triggers the dynamics of polarization. The idea of an "apocalypse"—an imminent end and judgment of the world, separating humankind into friends and foes, saved and condemned, that arose at the same time as the first outbreaks of religious violence—exactly fulfills this condition of religious *Ernstfall*. Under these conditions, religion claims hegemony over the other spheres of culture, including politics, and becomes "total religion."

Although the dynamics of polarization and totalization under the auspices of an *Ernstfall* seem to be restricted to monotheism with its concept of absolute, revealed truth, there is no reason why truth should necessarily turn to violence. Since the eighteenth century, and building on older traditions such as the "parable of the rings," ways have been devised to overcome the innate intolerance of truth and its polarizing effects.

1

STRUCTURE AND CHANGE IN ANCIENT EGYPTIAN RELIGION

I n 1967, Siegfried Morenz, a renowned specialist in ancient Egyptian religion, published a lecture in which he set out what he called "the structure of Egyptian religion."[1] His definition consisted in positioning Egyptian religion within three pairs of oppositions: defining it as a national religion, not a world religion; a cult religion, not a book religion; and a historically developed religion, not a founded religion. This definition amounts to identifying Egyptian religion as a "primary" religion in contrast to "secondary religions," which are defined as founded religions, all of which are *eo ipso* book religions and world religions.[2] This definition of ancient Egyptian religion is of course very unspecific. It lumps Egyptian religion together with all other primary religions without, however, identifying any of its specific traits within this immensely broad field. Moreover, it leaves the general notion of 'religion' undefined. Any attempt at determining the specificity of ancient Egyptian religion should start with a rough definition of religion as the common denominator, and then proceed to determine the specific differences characteristic of Egyptian religion within this field.

What is religion? I shall try to answer this question by pointing to what it is about. Religion, in my view, comprises three fields of human action and thought: cult, theology, and lifestyle.[3] Any religion deserving of the name should be able to answer questions concerning its forms of cult, its implicit or explicit concepts of the divine, and its impact on the lifestyle of its members. Even at this fundamental level, we should be prepared to meet huge differences among religions. There are some, among them the ancient Egyptian religion, where the cult holds the central and most prominent place; others, such as Christianity, have their center in theology; and still others, such as Judaism and Buddhism, are primarily

7

concerned with questions of lifestyle. Nevertheless, all three dimensions should be expressed in some way or other in any of these religions, and ancient Egypt proves to be rather prolific in texts and other phenomena concerning theology and lifestyle, as well as cult, which forms its dominating center. A religion gets its specific profile by its forms and fields of emphasis within this triad of cult, theology, and lifestyle.

Cult

Cult is about contact with the divine or the holy or whatever we would like to call this other sphere of reality. The universally most important form of coming into contact with it is gift-giving or sacrifice. As the Latin, French, and English words 'sacrificere,' 'sacrifier,' 'to sacrifice' show, to sacrifice is *the* sacred action par excellence. Sacrifice is communication by giving. It means a kind of giving that is not only an enrichment for the receiver, but also a serious renunciation or abandonment for the donor. The gift must be precious in order to achieve the desired effects of communication, the most important of which is atonement, reconciliation, or satisfaction. The Egyptian word for sacrifice, *hetep*, also means 'peace,' and the verb *se-hetep* means 'to reconcile,' 'to appease.'[4] The meaning of cult and ritual, in Egypt and in presumably all other primary religions, is to reconcile human society with the divine world, to integrate human life into the processes and cycles of cosmic life that are conceived of as the divine world, and to maintain the cosmos by assisting the gods in overcoming chaos. Three properties define the specificity of Egyptian religion in this field of sacred action: the role of 'magic,' the divinity of the ruler, and the importance of the mortuary cult.

Maintaining cosmic order is the most important goal of cultic action, and it requires magical power. There is, therefore, no way of distinguishing between 'religion' and 'magic' in ancient Egypt. Magic is religion and vice versa—at least, magic is the center of the cult and the cult is the center of Egyptian religion. There is no word in Egyptian that we could translate as 'religion,' but there are two words that we cannot translate otherwise than as 'magic': *heka* and *akhu*. Magic, in Egypt, means the operation of cosmogonic energies for the purpose of maintaining or restoring order. The energies which were once active in creating the world are still active in maintaining it, and human society is able, even obliged, to partake in this task of maintaining the universe. This idea of maintenance or restoration extends from the cosmic to the private sphere, from assisting the sun god to overcome darkness and to traverse the sky and the netherworld to assisting a patient to overcome the evil influence of some malignant demon and to handle the crisis of death. This concept of cult and magic is very common among primary religions; if there is anything specifically Egyptian in this respect, it is the role of language and the proliferation of texts to be recited during the performance of cultic action. These texts are highly specific and there is much to learn from Egyptian texts about the meaning of cultic action. For an example, I would mention the principle of 'sacramental interpretation,' whereby every action must be accompanied by a spell that expresses its sacramental meaning with reference to the divine world. Giving bread and beer to the dead, for example, may be interpreted as assisting the dead to ascend to heaven and to unite with the sun god.[5]

The divinity of the ruler assures the link between the divine world and human society. The Egyptian idea of cult as communication with the divine is not, as one might expect, between humans and gods, but about gods and gods. The priest, or, more generally, everybody who is qualified in operating cosmogonic powers, has to play the role of a god or to act as a representative of a god. This system of representation is founded on the idea that the king is a god incarnate and that he is able to delegate aspects of his divinity to officiants acting on his behalf or in his name. Sacred kingship is a very widespread idea, but the Egyptian concept of pharaoh as a god on earth and the son of the highest god is extreme in its emphasis on the divinity of the ruler.[6] This means that, in Egypt, "reigning" counts among the sacred actions. Reigning is another way of operating cosmogonic energies. It is the continuation of creation under the conditions of the existing world. The person, or the office, of the king assures the continuity between the divine and the human world and between cosmogony and present time. The most important aspect of ruling, and the primary role of the king, is to establish and to maintain contact with the divine world. In the execution of his official role, he is himself a god, the only one on earth qualified for conversing with the gods, but he delegates this office to the priesthoods of the various deities and their local cults. As an important text specifies, his role is to establish *ma'at*—order, harmony, justice—on earth by "judging mankind and satisfying the gods."[7] Judging mankind is explained as rescuing the weak and poor from the powerful and rich, and satisfying the gods is defined as giving offerings to the gods and to the dead.

This leads to the third point, after magic and sacred kingship: the central importance of the mortuary cult. In Egypt, the dead—on condition that they have reached the status of *akh* (transfigured spirit or the like)—count among the receivers of cult and sacrifice; one may even say that they belong to the divine sphere. While there is a difference between gods and spirits—*netjeru* and *akhu*—both belong to the other sphere which can only be reached by sacrifice, or 'sacred action' in the broadest sense. The similarity between divine and mortuary ritual is striking. The basic idea of reconciliation is the same. This seems to be another peculiarity that sets Egyptian religion off from other religions. The exceptional role of the dead, in Egypt, invites us to distinguish yet a third basic sacred action in addition to sacrificing and reigning, which is burying. Burying (in the broadest sense, including embalmment, mummification, and other funerary rituals), in Egypt, means transforming a dead person into a transfigured spirit. It is a kind of ritual deification, requiring, as one might imagine, a very special kind and amount of magical power or cosmogonic energy.[8]

Theology

If we now turn to the second domain of religion, the conceptions about the divine, which I subsume under the term 'theology,' I propose to distinguish between implicit and explicit theology and to concentrate on explicit theology. Let me first explain the distinction.[9] By 'implicit theology,' I mean the concepts about the divine that form the presupposition of cultic action. There is no practice without theory, and implicit theology is the theory implied in cultic practice. 'Explicit theology,' on the other hand, is a discourse about god and the gods that unfolds in a variety of textual genres and is independent of any cultic action. Explicit theology evolves around problems concerning the nature of the divine. The Egyptian theology, implicit as well as explicit, can be characterized as a 'cosmogonic monotheism'; the texts insist on the divine origin of the world and on the oneness of this origin. It is One God from whom the world originated, in the form both of emanation and of creation as complementary ways of emergence. The oneness of transcendent origin and the plurality of immanent manifestation are two dialectically related aspects of the world, with explicit theology focusing on the aspect of cosmogonic unity, implicit theology on that of manifest plurality. The first texts that may be classified as explicit theology deal with the problem of "justifying the ways of God," as Milton called it, the problem of theodicy. A prominent example forms the close of the instruction for King Merikare, dating probably from the early second millennium BCE[10] and belonging to wisdom literature, thus to a comparatively "secular" context far removed from cult. Wisdom literature, in Egypt, pertains more to the third domain of religion, "lifestyle" or moral philosophy.

Humans are well cared for,
the livestock of God;
he made heaven and earth for their sake.
He pushed back the greediness of the waters
and created the air so that their nostrils might live.
His images are they, having come forth from his body.

For their sake he rises to heaven.
For them he made plants and animals,
birds and fish,
so that they might have food.
If he killed his enemies and went against his children,
this was only because they thought of rebellion.

For their sake he causes there to be light.
To see them he travels [the heavens].
He established for himself a chapel at their back.
When they weep, he hears.
He created for them a ruler in the egg
and a commander to strengthen the backbone of the weak.

He made for them magic as a weapon
to ward off the blow of happenings.
Watching over them night and day,
he thrashed the crooked-hearted among them
as a man beats his son for the sake of his brother.
God knows every name.[11]

Remarkable about this text, first of all, is the fact that it speaks of "God" as if there were only one. This kind of monotheism, however, is not a matter of religion, but of genre and perspective. If one looks at the world in the way this text does, the principles of plurality and differentiation disappear, and the ultimate unity of the divine appears. This perspective is characteristic of the genre of wisdom literature, a forerunner of moral philosophy that reflects in a very general way on the fundamentals of human existence. Egyptian wisdom literature generally speaks of "God" instead of specific gods.[12] However, this is not merely a generic term, to be filled in by the name of a specific god in a given case ("to whom it may concern," that is, "a" god instead of "God"), but a specific term referring to the sun god and creator, who in all periods of pharaonic history was seen as the sole origin of the world and the highest god. In the perspective of moral philosophy, this is the only god that really counts, the one god on whom everything else (including the other gods) depends. Such a "monotheism of perspective" is conventionally termed 'henotheism.'[13] In Egypt, the henotheistic perspective of wisdom literature and the polytheism of cult coexist without any apparent conflict. During the New Kingdom, however, the henotheistic perspective starts to affect certain domains of temple literature as well, especially hymns to Amun-Re, the god of the capital, Thebes, who becomes identified with the sun god of Heliopolis. Thus, another problem of theology arises, which is the relationship between this one highest god and the multitude of other gods. An early hymn to Amun-Re, dating back perhaps to a time even before the New Kingdom, adopts the anthropocentric and henotheistic perspective of Merikare.

Hail, Re, lord of justice,
who chapel is hidden, lord of the gods;
Khepry in his boat
at whose command the gods emerge;
Atum, creator of human beings,
who differentiates them and makes them live,
who distinguishes people by the color of their skin,
who hears the prayers of those in distress
and is well disposed to those who call on him,
who rescues the fearful from the overbearing,
who judges between rich and poor.
Lord of perception, on whose lips is the creative word,
it is for his sake that Hapy (the inundation) has come;
lord of sweetness, great of love,
it is to make people live that he has come.[14]

To be sure, the gods, plural, are mentioned in other sections of this text, which is still a far cry from real monotheism and even henotheism. However, as Eric Voegelin writes: "In all polytheism is latent a monotheism which can be activated at any time."[15] In Egypt, this latent monotheism gained more and more momentum in the course of the New Kingdom and became overwhelmingly manifest with the religious revolution of Akhenaten, who quite simply did away with the plurality of gods and abolished traditional religion altogether. This single event, which overturned traditional religion in Egypt in the most fundamental way, proves the eminent place held by theology in ancient Egyptian religion. Akhenaten's revolution implemented the henotheistic perspective in terms of cult and religious institutions, turning the sun and creator god into the sole and only god, and denying the other gods any worship and even existence.[16] In the aftermath of this revolutionary step, the gods were readmitted into theology; the henotheistic perspective, however, still prevailed, and the gods, especially in hymns to Amun, tended now to be demoted to "names," "manifestations," "symbols," "limbs," and the like, of the One.

The culmination of these tendencies was reached when the whole pantheon came to be seen as just aspects of one supreme god. "All gods are three," we read in an Egyptian text, which then states that these three gods are just aspects of One God:

All gods are three:
Amun, Re, and Ptah, whom none equals.
He who hides his name as Amun,
he appears to the face as Re,
his body is Ptah.[17]

All gods are three, and these three are encompassed and transcended by a god who is referred to only as "He," whose name is Amun, whose cosmic manifestation is Re, and whose body, or cult image, is Ptah. Even the name of "Amun," the "Hidden One," is just an epithet screening the true and hidden name of this god, of whom another hymn states:

People fall down immediately for fear
if his name is uttered knowingly or unknowingly.
There is no god able to call him by it.[18]

This text was written in the thirteenth century, when the monotheistic revolution by Akhenaten had already been overturned and the traditional religion with its plethora of temples and deities was reinstituted. Despite this external restitution, however, Akhenaten's revolution had left a deep impression on Egyptian thought and had led to a veritable explosion of explicit theological discourse, which now concentrated more than ever on the topic of the oneness of God. The traditional paradigm of creation and sovereignty is now complemented by the new paradigm of hiddenness and manifestation.[19]

In contrast to the "paradigm of creation," the model of manifestation does not temporize the god–world relationship. The traditional concept of primacy has both a temporal and a hierarchical meaning. To be the first means to be the chief. The first contains in his essence, in a seminal way, all that comes later. Primacy means all-ness. The name 'Atum' means 'to be complete' in this very sense of primordial or preexistent primacy. By turning from creator to maintainer, however, the first and highest god has to resign, in a way, from his all-encompassing, all-absorbing, and omnipotent position in relation to the other gods. Creation turns into cooperation. Oneness is the quality of chaos or preexistence, whereas existence and cosmos are characterized by difference, diversity, antagonism, and cooperation. Maintenance is teamwork. The One must become a partner. The leading model for expressing the maintenance of the world in terms of cooperation and partnership is the mythology of the Solar Course, which shows the sun god sailing in a boat through the sky and the underworld, an action in which virtually all of the gods take part.[20] This cyclical process is both a process of biological regeneration, in which the sun god passes through the phases of day and night as a newborn child, a young man, an old man, and a dead person, and a process of political triumph, in which the sun god is continuously defeating Apopis, the personification of chaos. In both aspects —being subject to periodic death and rebirth, and being confronted by a counter-power of chaos—the sun god as maintainer of the world differs from the sun god as creator of the world in that he himself becomes dependent, becomes integrated into a system of interdependence.

During the Eighteenth Dynasty, this traditional cooperative model of the solar circuit had already started to give way to a different model, whose main tendency was to increase the distance between god and gods or god and the world.[21] Now the sun god is no longer shown as a partner in a cooperative action, embedded in varying constellations of gods, submitted to the sequence of life and death, and confronted by a counteracting foe. Rather, he circulates around the world on a solitary course and maintains the world in a way that is very similar, if not identical, to primordial creation. This leads to a certain de-temporization of the concept of divine oneness, which is no longer restricted to chaos and preexistence, but becomes connected to the sun in relation and opposition to the world. Thus, in a sun hymn on a pre-Amarna stela, we read:

> You have settled very remote,
> very far away;
> you have revealed yourself in heaven in your aloneness.
> Every god on earth,
> their arms are held out in praise at your rising.
> You shine, and they see,
> they raise themselves, their arms bent in respect before your display
> of power.[22]

In this and several other texts dating from the time preceding the Amarna revolution, the traditional constellations of deities have disappeared. The god confronts the world in sublime solitude. The distance between god and world has become extreme. Akhenaten's revolution is a radicalization of this concept. His innovations include: (1) the complete disappearance of the many gods, who, in the stage of solar theology immediately preceding the Amarna revolution, belong to the world which the sun god creates and maintains; (2) the complete elimination of the topic of creation, thus a radical de-temporization of the relationship between god and world; and (3) a "pantheistic" concept of continuous creation and participation, using the term *kheperu*, 'transformations.'

> You create millions of forms *(kheperu)* from yourself, the One,
> Cities and towns
> Fields, paths and river.[23]

The "million *kheperu*" obviously refer to the visible world in its aspect of a space made habitable by light and ordered in the form of a cosmos. Yet another hymn opposes the One and the Millions as aspects of God himself:

You made heaven remote to rise in it
To see all that you created, you being alone.
But there being millions of lives in you (for you) to make them live.[24]

The paradigm of manifestation was developed in reaction to Akhenaten's radical monotheism. In the same way as Akhenaten's opposition of god and world, this new paradigm de-temporizes the relation between god and world; the difference lies in the fact that the gods are now readmitted into the world and that the relation between god and world is interpreted also in terms of a relation between god and gods, the one and the many. In the paradigm of manifestation, God does not resign from his sublime Oneness in creating or becoming the world. In order to explain the new conception of the relationship between god and world, the theologians avail themselves of an anthropological concept, the concept of *ba*, which we conventionally translate as 'soul.' God remains One in relating to the world, similarly to the way in which the *ba* relates to the body, an invisible, animating principle. From this concept follow two theological assumptions that will play an important role in Hellenism: God is the soul of the world and the world is the body of God. As the *ba*, the soul animating the world, God is nameless and hidden, a *deus absconditus*:

He is *ba*-like, hidden of name like his secrecy.[25]

Thus we read in a hymn of pLeiden I 350. The *ba* theology preserves Akhenaten's de-temporized concept of Oneness by further elaborating his model of manifestation, for which Akhenaten had made ample use of the term *kheperu* ('transformation'), and Akhnenaten's opposition of One-and-millions, for which Ramesside theology coins the formula for God as "the One who transforms/transformed himself into millions."

Hail to you, the One who transforms himself into millions,
Whose length and breadth are limitless![26]
Power in readiness, who gave birth to himself,
Uraeus with great flame;
Great of magic with secret form,
Secret *ba*, to whom respect is shown.[27]

The opposing terms "One" and "millions" are linked here by the concept of self-transformation: *jrj sw*, 'who made or makes himself into.' "Millions" clearly refers to the world of creation, which is interpreted as a transformation of God himself. Creation is emanation. The world is created not out of chaos or *prima materia*, nor *ex nihilo*, out of nothing, but *ex Deo*, out of God. God is limitless; so is the world; God is the world. The following verses oppose two aspects of God, *sekhem seped*, 'power in readiness,' and *ba sheta'*, 'secret *ba*,' the first referring to the sun, and the second referring to the hidden aspect of God as a soul animating the world from within. In Amarna, the One is the sun, the absolutely and overwhelmingly manifest and visible god, opposite to and animating the world, which has no divinity of its own. In Ramesside Thebes, the One is the absolutely hidden and secret *ba* animating the world from within. Thus, Ramesside theology is able both to retain and to surpass the Amarna idea of Oneness.

In this context, the formula of One-and-millions returns frequently and in a number of variants. The "millions" are stated to be god's body,[28] his limbs,[29] his transformation,[30] and even his name: "million of millions is his name."[31] By transforming himself into a million-fold reality, God has not ceased to be a unity. He is both one and millions, unity and plurality, hidden and present at the same time, in that mysterious way which this theology is trying to grasp by means of the *ba* concept.

As *ba*, God is the hidden power that manifests itself in the world. However, these manifestations may also be called *ba*. A "magical" text from the Saite period distinguishes seven *ba* manifestations of Amun.

The Bes with seven heads . . .
He is (embodies) the *ba*s of Amun-Re, lord of Karnak, chief of Ipet-Sut,
The ram with sublime face, who dwells in Thebes.
The great lion who generated by himself,
The great god of the beginning,
The ruler of lands and the king of gods,
The lord of heaven, earth, underworld, water, and mountains
Who conceals his name from the gods,
The giant of millions of cubits,
The strong . . . who fixed the sky on his head,
From whose nose the air comes forth,
In order to animate all noses,

Who rises as sun, in order to illuminate the earth,
From whose bodily secretions the Nile flows forth in order to nourish
  every mouth.[32]

As an illustration of this theology, for which there are many examples, I
quote just one passage from a hymn in the tomb of Imiseba (TT 65) from
the time of Ramesses IX.

Your eyes are the sun and the moon,
your head is the sky,
your feet are the underworld.[33]

The idea of the world as the embodiment of a soul-like god and of
God as a soul animating the world remains central in Egyptian theology even after the New Kingdom and the flourishing of its theological
discourse. We are dealing here with the origin of a conception of the
divine which was to become supremely important in late antiquity: the
"cosmic god," the supreme deity in Stoicism, Hermeticism, and related
movements,[34]

whose head is the sky,
whose body is the air, whose feet are the earth.
You are the ocean.[35]

With this last quotation, we have entered another time and another
language. This text and many similar ones are in Greek and date from
late antiquity. They belong to a syncretistic religion combining elements
of Egyptian theology with Stoicism, Neoplatonism, and various other
influences.

In spite of all these changes, however, the theological discourse continues, and there is a remarkable consistency of questions and answers.
Their most explicit codification is to be found in the texts forming the
Corpus Hermeticum. The "pantheistic" motif of the One and the millions appears in the Greek texts as the One and the All, *to hen kai to
pan*, or *hen to pan*, and so on,[36] and in a Latin inscription for Isis as
una quae es omnia.[37] The "cosmotheistic" aspect is expressed in statements about the world as the body of God, such as in an oracle reported
by Macrobius:

The celestial universe is my head,
my body is the ocean,
the earth is my feet,
my ears are in the ether,
my far-shining eye is the light of Helios.[38]

The discourse of explicit theology arrives at a solution of the problem of how to correlate god and gods that may be summarized by the formula "All gods are One." This is the form of cosmotheistic and hypercosmic monotheism characteristic of Hellenistic and late antique religiosity, and which can also be found in Mesopotamian, Iranian, and Indian texts. Egypt, however, is the civilization where these ideas can be traced back to a much earlier age than elsewhere and where they can be explained as the result of a long development.

The importance of theology within the structure of ancient Egyptian religion cannot be overestimated. The enormous proliferation of important and highly original theological hymns, especially during the New Kingdom, the rapid evolution of ideas that took place within the theological discourse, and the range of their social and political consequences as shown by the Amarna revolution have scarcely any parallel in the ancient world before the rise of monotheism. Even in the Old Testament there are few texts that can compare with the most advanced theological hymns of Ramesside Egypt.

The Guidance of Life

The norms of leading a good life, or moral philosophy, is the point where ancient Egypt differs most from our modern concept of religion. Questions of how to lead a good life are dealt with, in Egypt, not in religious but in secular texts. The prescriptions of morality, such as to support the poor, widows, and orphans; to control one's greed, lust, and appetite; to obey one's superiors and to care for one's underlings—all these social norms, which in Egypt are referred to as "the laws of *ma'at*,"[39] are secular recommendations and not religious commandments. Lifestyle, in Egypt, is a secular, not a religious, concern. This situation changes only with the advent of personal piety and its reflection in the *Teachings of Amenemope*. To lead a good life does not mean to fulfill the will of God and does not bring one any closer to God, but it inscribes a person into the social memory of the community and assures him or her of a kind of immortality.

However, there is one exception to this rule, which is of the highest importance and which, by its rise and development, changed the structure of Egyptian religion in the most fundamental ways. This is the idea of a judgment after death.[40]

In the Old Kingdom, Pharaoh, being a god incarnate, was the only being who was granted real immortality and not merely endurance in social memory. Pharaoh was believed to ascend to heaven and unite with the gods. A plethora of rituals and recitation texts surrounded this ascension. The decisive transformation of Egyptian funerary beliefs came with the breakdown of the Old Kingdom when these rituals, texts, and beliefs became accessible to a greater number of people all over the country. At that point, the originally royal concept of afterlife lost its political meaning and was generalized and extended to virtually everybody. The distinction between royals and mortals was transformed into the distinction between good and bad, worthy and unworthy, just and unjust. This is how the concept of a judgment of the dead was born, which eventually transformed Egyptian religion into a precursor of later religions of salvation and which had such a great influence on Christianity and other religions.

The judgment of the dead brings about the "justification" of the dead. In the Old Kingdom, this idea was ritually staged in the form of the Osiris myth. Osiris had to be justified against his brother Seth, who had murdered him. This justification took the form of a lawsuit between Horus, the son of Osiris, and Seth about the succession to the throne of Egypt. The deceased king plays the role of Osiris, his son and successor the role of Horus. Seth, his mythical adversary, personifies the death that the deceased has suffered.

This is the mythical model of the pharaonic victory over death as it was acted out in the royal funerary cult of the Old Kingdom. After the end of the Old Kingdom, the mythical model of death underwent a process of moralization and gave way to the "moral model," according to which everybody is believed to appear after death before a divine tribunal, not as an accuser but as a defendant. The victory over death is now no longer conceived of as justification *against* an enemy, but as justification *before* a divine judge. But the Egyptians never completely did away with older concepts; they retained the mythical model of the justification against Seth, but they turned it into a symbol for the justification before God. Death, in mythical thought, was considered a crime that must be vindicated. There is guilt behind every death, and this guilt has to be removed in order to restore the deceased to status and position in society. In the "moralized" version of justification, death is still conceived of as associated with guilt, but now it is the guilt of the deceased himself that must be removed in order to restore him or her to life and status. In the funerary liturgies of the Middle Kingdom, the texts dealing with the judgment after death form part of the ritual of embalmment and mummification. After the purification and preservation of the body, the embalmment and mummification ritual turns in its last stage to the soul, that is, to the spiritual aspects or components of the person. The primary purpose of the judgment is to purge the soul of guilt. Guilt is interpreted as a kind of immaterial pollutant causing death and corruption of the moral self, much in the same way as the bodily pollutants which the embalmment ritual seeks to remove might cause death and corruption of the bodily self. "Separating a man from all the sins that he may have committed" is the title of the recitation in its classical form.

As long as the idea of a judgment after death remained confined to the frame of ritual, we cannot be sure about its relevance for the questions of lifestyle. In order for it to become a moral concept, the idea should extend far beyond the confines of funerary ritual and turn into a fundamental ethical principle informing the whole moral orientation of the society. A first hint of this direction is given by the same text from which we have already quoted an early text of explicit theology, the *Instructions for King Merikare*.

> The court that judges the wretch,
> You know they are not lenient
> On the day of judging the miserable,
> In the hour of doing their task.
> It is painful when the accuser has knowledge.
>
> Do not trust in length of years.
> They view a lifetime in an hour!
> When a man remains over after death,
> His deeds are set beside him as a sum.
>
> Being yonder lasts forever.
> A fool is he who does what they reprove!

He who reaches them without having done wrong
Will exist there like a god,
free-striding like the lords of eternity![41]

Here we are clearly dealing with a concept of great importance, not only for the afterlife, but even for life on earth. The question of whether or not one reaches the lords of eternity is not decided by the performance of a ritual but by a good life.

In the course of this development from a ritualistic concept into a fundamental idea of immense importance and influence for individual and social life, it must have become more and more necessary to know the norms and requirements on the basis on which the judges would form their judgment. What was needed was, to use a Jewish comparison, a kind of Egyptian "Torah" on which to found an Egyptian *halakha*—that is, a lifestyle that corresponds to the criteria of divine judgment. The answer to this need is chapter 125 of the *Book of the Dead* (BD 125).

The great achievement of this text was that it made explicit the moral expectations of the judges. Now, with the rise of the New Kingdom and the recension of the *Book of the Dead*, the rules of admission into the other world had become codified. The mythical model of a lawsuit between Osiris and Seth had disappeared altogether. The whole procedure now more closely resembled an examination and an initiation.

The deceased had to present himself before Osiris, the president of the court, and before a jury of forty-two judges. He no longer had to be prepared to face accusations that any unspecified accuser could bring forward against him. He knew the accusations beforehand and had to protest his innocence concerning eighty-two sins that he affirmed not to have committed. During this recital, the heart of the candidate was weighed on a balance against a figure of Truth. Every lie would make the heart sink a little deeper on the scale. If the heart was found to be too heavy and irredeemably charged with guilt and lies, a monster, which is always shown close to the balance and watching the weighing, would swallow it and annihilate the culprit's person.

BD 125 belongs to the genre of funerary literature, meant to equip the dead with necessary knowledge. But nothing speaks against the assumption that this text was important for the living as well. We may safely assume that the judgment after death and the laws of the Hall of Truths not only decided the future destiny of the soul, but also determined to a certain degree the lifestyle of the living. There is even a text where a man protests that he has led a life in conformity with "the laws of the Hall of Truths," by which he obviously refers to the eighty-two protestations of innocence. This autobiographical inscription dating from the Eighteenth Dynasty (fifteenth or fourteenth century BCE) might well be representative of a general moral attitude in ancient Egypt.

> I have come to this town of eternity,
> having done good on earth.
> I did not rob, I was blameless,
> my name was not uttered for any mistake,
> nor any vileness and crime.
> To speak the truth was my delight,
> for I knew it profits its doer
> on earth from birth to landing.
> It is an effective guard for its speaker,
> on the day he arrives at the court
> that judges the distressed, discerns qualities,
> punishes the criminal, destroys his *ba*.
> I am without blame, I have no accuser!
> Without wrong before them, may I come out justified,
> and praised among the honored who joined their *kas*!
> . . .
>
> I am a noble and pleased with right,
> who conformed to the laws of the Hall of Truths,
> for I planned to reach the necropolis without baseness attached to
>   my name.[42]

This text starts with the declaration:

> I am one truly straight, free of wrongdoing,
> who put the god in his heart and is aware of his might.

"To put the god into one's heart" is the Egyptian formula for what in Egyptological parlance is called 'personal piety.' Personal piety is the form in which, in Ramesside Egypt, religion began to determine the individual lifestyle and moral orientation of humans in such decisive ways that even the wisdom literature of the time, the teachings of Amenemope above all, adopted this attitude.[43] *Ger ma'a* ('the truly silent') became the ideal of wisdom. It is a definition of *homo religiosus*, who humbly surrenders his life to the will of God. There is no room left for more than just an allusion to this arguably most decisive innovation in the history of Egyptian religion. Thus I offer one small example to illustrate this change. Before the Ramesside period, a usual epistolary formula was, "Today I am fine, but my state tomorrow I do not know." The later version said, "Today I am fine. Tomorrow lies in the hands of God."[44]

2

MYTH AND HISTORY OF THE EXODUS: TRIUMPH AND TRAUMA

The Mnemohistory of the Exodus

The Biblical story of the Exodus of the children of Israel from Egypt is probably the most influential story ever told. It is not only about the foundation of Judaism being annually retold and literally relived through every Seder night;[1] it also inspired revolutionary movements such as the Reformation, the Puritan revolt in England, and the emigration of the Puritans to America and the Boers to South Africa. It has also served as a symbol for movements of intellectual emancipation known as the Enlightenment, which Kant defined as "the Exodus of mankind from its self-imposed immaturity."[2] It is not only about the founding of a people (the people of God, the chosen people) serving as a model for all kinds of nation-building and political mythology, but also about the founding of a new religion, forming the model for the founding of later religions such as Christianity and Islam. Every founder of a new religion marched in the footsteps of Moses. The very idea that religions may be founded, based on the revelation of a higher truth that puts every existing religion and tradition in the position of untruth or error, is rooted in the myth of the Exodus from Egypt. The notion of redemption means first and foremost the redemption of the Israelites from Egyptian bondage, and came only in Christian reinterpretation to mean redemption from sin and death. And even for Christians, who no longer locate the Promised Land in Canaan or any other geographically localizable region but in the heavenly Jerusalem or the Kingdom of God, the idea of Exodus, of leaving the old life behind in order to follow Christ, has a poignant meaning.

Given this enormous radiance, it is small wonder that the story of *yitzi'at Mitzrayim*, the Exodus from Egypt, has always provoked questions about what really happened. The ancient Egyptian evidence was searched again and again for any traces that could confirm the Biblical record. Any new excavation, especially that of the tomb of Tutankhamun, was hailed with great expectations of a final proof. Theories have been formed about the causes of the ten plagues: Collision with a meteorite? A climate catastrophe because of the eruption of the Thera volcano? What could have caused the parting of the sea? A storm? Archaeology in Palestine focused on the goal of discovering traces of the conquest of Canaan that followed the emigration: Levels of destruction? A dramatic change of material culture? Jericho in particular has been investigated, with the sole discovery that the site was deserted in Biblical times and the destruction antedates by far the events recounted in the book of Joshua. In spite of all this desperate research, not a single trace has turned up that could shed light on what really happened.[3] Rather than asking what really happened, therefore, it is better to ask how this historically ungraspable event came to be remembered and to assume its enormous importance. This will be the aim of this chapter.

Let us set aside for a moment the question of what really happened and ask instead about who remembers, when, and why, following a Latin scholastic hexameter teaching how to flesh out an argument with historical circumstances:

Quís, quid, ubí, quibus aúxiliís, cur, quómodo, quándo?
Who?, what?, where?, by what means?, why?, how? and when?[4]

This is not to say that the story of the Exodus has no historical basis at all. On the contrary, there is a plethora of historical events and experiences that may have left their traces in the Biblical record: the expulsion of the Hyksos, Palestinian invaders who ruled Egypt for over a hundred years and were finally expelled around 1500 BCE;[5] the religious revolution of Akhenaten;[6] the experiences of the 'Apiru or Habiru (very probably = 'ibrîm 'Hebrews'), gangs of antisocial people operating between Egypt's vassal states and resisting Egyptian control, who could well have been taken into Egyptian captivity and have later escaped;[7] finally, the large-scale migrations of the "sea peoples" who caused unrest and turmoil in the eastern Mediterranean until eventually settling in Italy (Etruria, Sicily, Sardinia), Greece, Turkey, and Palestine, regions that bear their names even today.[8] The Exodus myth may have integrated these various memories into a coherent story that is fictional as to its composition but historical as to some of its components.

Who is first to tell the story? Where, why, how, and when?

The first allusion to the Exodus occurs with the early prophets Hosea, Micah, and Amos at the end of the eighth century BCE: "Did I not lead you out of Egypt and release you from bondage and send before you Moses, Aaron, and Miriam?" (Micah 6:4). "When Israel was a child, I loved him, and out of Egypt I called my son" (Hosea 11:1). "I brought you out of Egypt and led you forty years through the desert" (Amos 2:10).

Let us ask our mnemohistorical questions: Who? When? Why? *Who* were the prophets? They were early and passionate mono-Yahwists, as I would like to call them, preaching exclusive loyalty to Yahweh alone.[9] They were not monotheists, to be sure, because their concept of loyalty presupposes a world full of other gods whom Israel is all too prone to worship alongside Yahweh, a step that Hosea denounces as adultery.

When? At a time of utmost danger and affliction under the Assyrians. These prophets lived under the last kings of the Northern Kingdom and witnessed their desperate struggle between the two superpowers Assyria and Egypt.

Why? The meaning of their message is obvious: "Remember the past and trust in the future; only then will you overcome the dangerous present."

Another prophet who refers to the Exodus myth is Haggai. We read at the beginning of chapter 2 of his book:

> On the twenty-first day of the seventh month, the word of the LORD came through the prophet Haggai: "Speak to Zerubbabel son of Shealtiel, governor of Judah, to Joshua son of Jozadak, the high priest, and to the remnant of the people. Ask them, 'Who of you is left who saw this house in its former glory? How does it look to you now? Does it not seem to you like nothing? But now be strong, Zerubbabel,' declares the LORD. 'Be strong, Joshua son of Jozadak, the high priest. Be strong, all you people of the land,' declares the LORD, 'and work. For I am with you,' declares the LORD Almighty. 'This is what I covenanted with you when you came out of Egypt. And my Spirit remains among you. Do not fear.'" (Haggai 2:1–5)

With this passage, we are in another time and another situation. Haggai dates his vision to the year 520 BCE, on 17 October, thus more than two hundred years after Hosea. The catastrophe that Hosea saw coming has meanwhile happened, twice over, first to the Northern and then to the Southern Kingdom. Hosea reminded the people of the Exodus in order to warn them not to defect from the quasi-matrimonial relationship with their God; Haggai, by contrast, recalls the Exodus to encourage them to believe in the alliance with God and his promise. The Hebrew phrase *ha-ddavar asher karatti ittekhem* means literally 'the words that I *cut* with you.' In Hebrew, a covenant is "cut" between the two parties (similarly, in ancient Greek, the phrase *spondas temnein*, 'to cut a treaty,' is used for forming a contract). Hosea is a prophet of disaster, Haggai a prophet of hope and comfort.

About the same time as the prophet Hosea, the priests at Jerusalem composed the "Priestly Code," combining the books of Genesis and Exodus. Here, the events of the Exodus of the Israelites from Egypt are narrated in great detail. The answer to the question "Who tells the story?" can only be "the Jerusalem priesthood."[10] The answer to "When?" is clear: with the return of the exiles from Babylon, when the concept of Israel had to be reinvented and the cult had to be reestablished. "Why?" The story is told not for its own sake but for the sake of a new and revolutionary idea: the idea of the covenant (Hebrew *b'rît*) that God formed with his Chosen People. The core of the text forms the revelation or "gift" of the Law (Torah) to the people through the mediation of Moses on Mount Sinai and the central idea on behalf of which the story is told.

B'rît is a political concept, meaning a treaty of alliance formed either between sovereign states on a base of equality or between a suzerain and a vassal state.[11] God presents himself, in forming the covenant, as "Yahweh thy God who brought thee out of Egypt." He forms this alliance, not as the *creator* with mankind, but as the *liberator* with the group of the liberated. Most of the prescriptions and prohibitions that follow from the covenant and are listed in the book do not make any sense without the story of liberation that explains and determines them. A political alliance between a god and a people is an absolutely new, unheard of, and unprecedented concept. As such, it requires a certain amount of historical motivation and explanation. This is the reason why the story is told. We are dealing here not with just "a" story, but with "the" story, the foundation of the covenant that is the foundation of the people of Israel and of Jewish and Christian religion.

Narrative Structure

In the book of Exodus, the compact myth is unfolded in a sequence of core scenes:

(1) In Egypt: oppression and suffering of the Israelites; birth and youth of Moses; his flight to Midian (chapters 1–2)
(2) In Midian: Moses's calling to become the prophet of God and the savior of his people (chapters 3–4)
(3) In Egypt: Moses's and Aaron's negotiations with Pharaoh; the ten plagues (chapters 5–11)
(4) Passover and Exodus, the crossing of the *yam suph* (Red Sea) (chapters 12–15)
(5) In the wilderness: manna, quails, water, and "murmuring" (chapters 16–18)
(6) Sinai: the gift of the Torah (chapters 19–31)
(7) Sinai: crisis (the Golden Calf) and the building of the tabernacle *(mishkan)* (chapters 32–40)

This structure, as indicated by the changes of place (except 6 and 7, which share the same location but are clearly set off against each other by a change of theme), seems the most natural one. It points to a cyclical construction: 3–1–3, with 4, "Passover and Exodus," as the decisive turning point around which the story unfolds. There are clear correspondences between 1 and 7, 2 and 6, and 3 and 5. Scene 1 describes the suffering of the Israelites in a state of extreme destitution; 7 shows them, after the crisis of the golden calf, as restored to the status of the people of God who takes his "dwelling" *(mishkan)* among them. Scene 2 narrates the revelation of God to Moses in the burning bush, 6 the revelation of the Torah on Mount Sinai. Scene 3 describes the testing of the Egyptians by means of the ten plagues that force them finally to give in and let the Israelites go; 5 describes the trials of the Israelites by a sequence of hardships (hunger, thirst, fatigue, battle) as a kind of initiatory probation before they are admitted to the holy mountain and the proximity of God.

We are dealing here with a careful composition, with a beginning, a middle, and an end. The tabernacle is a perfect ending of the story, which could have ended here. This motif concludes the emergence of a new religion by describing its institution. It fulfills the promise of God to dwell among his people. We now understand perfectly well why this composition is called the "priestly code."

In Leviticus and Numbers, the story continues with scene 8: the forty years of wandering in the wilderness, more legislation, and more crises. The severest of these are the episode of the spies, leading to God's verdict to ban the present generation from entering the Promised Land (Numbers 13–14), and the scene at Shittim, the last stage before entering the Promised Land, where the Israelites accept the invitation of the Moabites to join in a feast of their god Ba'al Pe'or, and twenty-four thousand are slain by a plague because of this transgression (Numbers 25).

Deuteronomy is a summarizing recapitulation on the eve of Israel's crossing of the Jordan. The last scene (9), the conquest, is told in the book of Joshua, which is separated from the Torah proper and relegated to the second group of books, the Prophets. The Torah ends with the death of Moses. This is highly significant. The story that begins with the suffering of the children of Israel in the hands of the Egyptians ends, not with the conquest of Canaan, but with the death of Moses, turning the story into a biography of Moses. The narrative structure is determined by the correspondence of beginning and end in terms of "lack" and "lack liquidated."[12] The lack is clearly represented by the suffering of Israel in Egypt (scene 1). It is liquidated by the life work of Moses, who has turned a mass of slaves into the people of God and has instituted a covenant in the form of a law, a cult, and a temple (scene 7). The Israelites have achieved this status even before entering the Promised Land, and it is, therefore, independent of their dwelling there. The point of the narrative is not conquest—from destitution to possession—but liberation: from serfdom to freedom. The Bible is careful in drawing the distinction between savior (Moses) and conqueror (Joshua) and in assigning the conqueror to the second rank. The lasting achievement of Moses is the covenant that God has formed with him and his people. This goal is achieved on Mount Sinai, in the no-man's-land between Egypt and Palestine, especially with the construction of the tabernacle—significantly, a portable sanctuary—that ensures God's presence among his people. The covenant has only to be *remembered* in the Promised Land in order for the Israelites to enjoy the freedom that the liberation from Egyptian serfdom has bestowed on them. To be and to remain free means to stay within the covenant and its stipulations; to abandon the covenant means to fall into the hands of other slaveholders and symbolically to return to Egypt.

Perhaps the strangest and most remarkable section of the Exodus narrative is scene 3, the ten plagues. In the economy of the narrative, the scene fulfills two functions: it compensates the Israelites for their suffering by punishing their tormentors, the Egyptians, and it makes clear beyond any doubt that the Israelites have not been *expelled* but *delivered* from Egypt. Nevertheless, one major plague would have fulfilled this function. Why ten of them? And why this sequence, which does not show a clear climactic logic?

1. turning the water of the Nile into blood
2. frogs
3. lice
4. insects
5. pestilence striking livestock
6. boils afflicting humans and beasts
7. hail smiting humans, beasts, and plants
8. locusts
9. darkness
10. killing of the firstborn

The multiplication of the motif of the plague by the factor ten has a clear mnemonic function. Like the Ten Commandments, it is based on human hands with their ten fingers. However, the plagues are not grouped, like the fingers and the Ten Commandments, into five and five (the Jewish division of the commandments), but by linguistic markers, such as introductory formulae, into triads.[13] The tenth plague, the killing of the firstborn, is set apart by a totally different form of narration; we shall return to this.

Plague	Forewarning	Time	Instruction	Agent
blood	yes	morning	"Station yourself"	Aaron
frogs	yes	—	"Go to Pharaoh"	Aaron
lice	no	—	—	Aaron
insects	yes	morning	"Station yourself"	God
pestilence	yes	—	—	God
boils	no	—	—	Moses
hail	yes	morning	"Station yourself"	Moses
locusts	yes	—	"Go to Pharaoh"	Moses
darkness	no	—	—	Moses
firstborn	yes	—	—	God

The plagues are *signs* to be remembered. This may explain their number. It is not one punishing and liberating event; it is a message to be forever retained and taken to heart.

The motif of the ten plagues elaborates the aspect of triumph, corresponding to the aspect of trauma by which the book begins: the genocidal suffering of the Israelites under Pharaoh. The narrative of the Exodus proper starts with trauma and ends with triumph, the most exultant expression of which is the song of Moses in chapter 15, unforgettably set to music by George Frideric Handel as the third part of his oratorio *Israel in Egypt*.

We must not forget, however, that the story is told in a post-traumatic situation. In the context of the books of Torah and historiography (Joshua, Judges, 1 and 2 Samuel, 1 and 2 Kings) that came to be written at the end of the sixth century, Exodus forms the first act, so to speak, of a drama unfolding in five acts. Exodus leads to the sealing of the covenant at Mount Sinai. This leads to the conquest of Canaan, and the centuries of living in Canaan, with all its inevitable compromises, end in the catastrophe of the destruction of Jerusalem and the Babylonian exile: Exodus—Covenant—Conquest—Kingdom(s)—Catastrophe. The books that codify the story are compiled after the fifth act, that is, after the return to Jerusalem under Persian rule. The real trauma behind this process of coming to terms with and reconstruction of the past is the fall of the kingdom of Judah, the destruction of the temple, and the fifty years of exile—the complete failure of the promise. A new beginning and a renewal of the promise can only succeed under the condition of integrating the apparently meaningless, catastrophic recent past into a broader view of sacred history—that is, by means of a feat of memory.

Remember the Exodus

The theme of memory is central in the tradition about the Exodus from Egypt. As a historical narrative, the book of Exodus is in itself an act of memory. It remembers an event of the past that, according to Biblical chronology, took place in the fifteenth century BCE, thus in the Late Bronze Age. The eighth and seventh centuries were generally a time of looking back across the break that the end of the Bronze Age and the first centuries of the Iron Age had brought about in the Mediterranean and Near Eastern world. In Egypt, this was a period of a very pronounced archaism. Texts were copied, and architectural, sculptural, and pictorial models were carefully followed, that date back to the second and third millennia BCE.[14] The Neo-Assyrian Empire looked back to the time of the Sargonid Empire of 1,500 years earlier as a golden age and a model of cultural and political perfection.[15] In Greece, the Homeric epics told the story of the Trojan war five hundred years before. This was a time of general reorientation, where the past began to matter in various conspicuous forms as a "normative past" that must by all means be remembered and followed as a source of political, legal, religious, and artistic models and norms. For Israel, the Exodus fulfilled precisely this function of a normative past. However, there is a decisive difference: Israel not only looked back like its neighbors, it also looked forward. The story of the Exodus is a story of promise. The covenant at Mount Sinai looks back to the Exodus from Egypt and forward to a blessed future in the Promised Land and in union with God—on the condition of the Israelites adhering faithfully to the covenant and its 613 statutes, commandments, and prohibitions. All depends on this one condition: that the covenant will not be neglected or broken.

In order to secure the keeping of the covenant, a mnemotechnique must be devised. This corresponds to traditional usage. Treaties have to be laid down in writing on durable material, such as a silver tablet to be deposited in the temple but also—and this is crucial—to be read aloud at regular intervals before the parties concerned. The Assyrian king Esarhaddon devised yet another ritual of commemoration. He summoned his subjects and vassals to the capital in order to swear an oath of loyalty to his designated successor Assurbanipal. Foreseeing, however, that the change of frame, when the subjects and vassals return to their homes, will cause them to forget, Esarhaddon devised a mnemonic ritual:

> Water from a *sarsaru* jar, she [Ishtar] gave them to drink,
> A goblet she half-filled with water from the *sarsaru* jar and gave it to
>   them, saying:
> You speak in your heart: Ishtar, a narrow one ['watchful' or 'locally
>   restricted'?] is she.
> But then you will go away to your towns and your districts,
> You will eat bread and forget these oaths.
> But as soon as you drink from this water,
> You will remind yourself and you will keep this swearing-in which I
>   have enacted on behalf of king Esarhaddon.[16]

The mnemotechnique that Moses devised in order to constantly remind the people of the covenant, its various obligations, and the story that frames and explains it, is laid out in Deuteronomy, the testament of Moses.[17] Deuteronomy prescribes *how* to remember *(quomodo, quibus auxiliis)*, but Exodus narrates *what (quid)* to remember. This mnemotechnique far surpasses anything comparable in the ancient world. Like Esarhaddon, Moses foresees that the people will forget their obligations once they live in the Promised Land, eat bread, and become sated.

> And it shall be when the LORD thy God shall have brought thee into the land he swore unto thy fathers . . . to give thee great and goodly cities which thou didst not build . . . houses full of all good things which thou didst not fill, then having eaten and been filled, . . . beware lest thou forget the LORD which brought thee forth out of the land of Egypt, from the house of bondage. (Deut. 6:10–12)

> Take heed to thyself that thou forget not the LORD thy God, so as not to keep his commands, and his judgments, and ordinances, which I command thee this day: lest when thou hast eaten and art full, and hast built goodly houses, and dwelt in them . . . thou shouldest be exalted in heart, and forget the LORD thy God, who brought thee out of the land of Egypt, out of the house of bondage. (Deut. 8:11–14)

Moses's mnemotechnique contains no fewer than seven different mnemonic devices:

1. Learning the text of the covenant by heart.
2. Teaching and explaining it to one's children, constantly discussing it, at home and away, by day and by night.[18]
3. Creating visible markers *(tefillin)*, to be worn on the body: "And thou shalt bind them for a sign upon thine hand, and they shall be as frontlets between thine eyes" (6:8).
4. Similarly, markers affixed to the doorposts *(mezuzot)*: "And thou shalt write them upon the posts of thy house, and on thy gates" (6:9).
5. Promulgation by public inscription: The canonized "words" *(debarim)* of the Law are to be written on plastered stelae to be set up immediately on entering the Promised Land. "And it shall be on the day

when ye shall pass over Jordan unto the land which the LORD thy God giveth thee, that thou shalt set thee up great stones, and plaster them with plaster. And thou shalt write upon them all the words of this law, when thou art passed over, that thou mayest go in unto the land which the LORD thy God giveth thee, a land that floweth with milk and honey; as the LORD God of thy fathers hath promised thee" (27:2–3).

6. Celebrating the three commemorative fests, Pesach, Shavuot, and Sukkot, all of which provide a frame for collective commemoration of the sojourn in Egypt, the Exodus, and the Torah. Concerning Passover it is said: "That thou mayest remember the day when thou camest forth out of the land of Egypt all the days of thy life" (16:3); concerning Shavuot: "And thou shalt remember that thou wast a bondsman in Egypt" (16:12); and Sukkot commemorates the nomadic life in the desert (16:13–15; cf. Leviticus 23:42–43). Moreover, it is stipulated that every seventh year the whole text of the Torah shall be read aloud to the people during Sukkot (31:10–13).

7. The seventh device concerns oral poetry. Moses teaches the Israelites a song dealing with the event of the Exodus, which they are commanded to learn by heart and to hand down orally to future generations (ch. 32).

This sevenfold mnemotechnique is sealed by a formula of closure and canonization: nothing must be added to nor subtracted from the commandments (Deut 4:2, 13:1[19]).

The Biblical story of the Exodus is, therefore, not only a *feat* of memory—remembering a profoundly decisive event of the distant past—but also and above all the *foundation* of a memory, part and object of a mnemotechnique that frames and supports the covenant. The Exodus is *the* decisive memory, never to fall into oblivion, and the book of Exodus is the codification of that memory. "Remember the Exodus" means "remember the covenant" and vice versa. To remember the Exodus and the covenant means always to remember the promise, to look into the future.

As stated above, the Mosaic mnemotechnique is laid out, not in Exodus but in Deuteronomy. Yet the book of Exodus also contains instructions for a ritual of commemoration. This is found in chapter 12, following the report of the tenth plague, the killing of the first-born in Egypt.

The LORD said to Moses and Aaron in Egypt, "This month is to be for you the first month, the first month of your year. Tell the whole community of Israel that on the tenth day of this month each man is to take a lamb for his family, one for each household. . . . [On] the fourteenth day of the month, all the members of the community of Israel must slaughter them at dusk. Then they are to take some of the blood and put it on the sides and tops of the door frames of the houses where they eat the lambs. That same night they are to eat the meat roasted over the fire, along with bitter herbs, and bread made without yeast. . . . Do not leave any of it till morning; if some is left till morning, you must burn it. This is how you are to eat it: with your cloak tucked into your belt, your sandals on your feet, and your staff in your hand. Eat it in haste; it is the LORD's Passover. . . .

"This is a day you are to commemorate; for the generations to come you shall celebrate it as a festival to the LORD—a lasting ordinance. For seven days you are to eat bread made without yeast. On the first day remove the yeast from your houses, for whoever eats anything with yeast in it from the first day through the seventh must be cut off from Israel. On the first day hold a sacred assembly, and another one on the seventh day. Do no work at all on these days, except to prepare food for everyone to eat; that is all you may do.

"Celebrate the Festival of Unleavened Bread, because it was on this very day that I brought your divisions out of Egypt. Celebrate this day as a lasting ordinance for the generations to come."[20]

In the same way as the *sarsaru* ritual is a ritual of drinking water, reminding the drinkers of the oath they have sworn, the Passover is a ritual of eating unleavened bread that reminds the eaters of their hasty departure from Egypt when they had no time to add yeast to their dough. For the same commemorative reason, the ritual has to be performed in the family and not in the synagogue, because the Israelites spent this night in their homes when the killing angel of the Lord struck the houses of the Egyptians.

The Seder Liturgy
In later times, in the diaspora, this ritual prescription has been fleshed out in great detail in the form of the Seder liturgy.[21] In the Jewish tradition, the memory of the Exodus lives on in two forms: (1) as part of synagogal recitation where the entire Torah is read in weekly portions (*parashot*) in

the course of the year, and (2) in the form of an annual celebration taking place not in the synagogue but at home, the *paterfamilias* (and not the rabbi) acting as master of ceremonies. Moses is scarcely mentioned in the Seder liturgy. This is the biggest difference between the book of Exodus, where Moses is the protagonist, and the myth of the Exodus, as reenacted in the Seder ceremony.

The Jewish Seder, the first night of Pesach, is the festive and liturgical realization of the commandment "Thou shalt teach your son and your son's son" that we were slaves in Egypt and that the Lord redeemed us from bondage with a strong hand and an outstretched arm. It is a "teach-in" to remember the connection between history and covenant, law and liberation. The story must be told and the questions must be asked in the "we" and "us" key. Why do we perform these rites and obey these laws? Because we were slaves in Egypt. In the same way as this "we" includes every Jew in addition to those who once emigrated from Egypt 3,500 years ago, the concepts of 'Egypt' and 'Pharaoh' extend to every form of oppression and violence wherever and whenever they occur. A Jew is someone who was liberated from Egypt and who is free insofar as he commits him/ herself to the covenant and its prescriptions. In liturgical memory, history is turned into myth, into a set of archetypal patterns with regard to which the present is made transparent so that these patterns shine through and render the present readable. As *The New York Times* put it some years ago:

> For thousands of years, Jews have affirmed that by participating in the Passover Seder, we not only remember the Exodus, but actually relive it, bringing its transformative power into our own lives.[22]

This is an excellent definition of liturgical memory. "In every generation," the Pesach Haggadah prescribes, "a man should look upon himself as if he came forth from Egypt."[23] The Seder teaches identity through identification. It is about the transformation of history into memory, to make a certain past "our" past and to let everyone participate in or even identify with this past as "his/her" past. One could even go so far as to speak of a transformation of semantic memory, something we have learned, into episodic memory, something we have lived, albeit in the form of a ritual play, of an "as if."

The function of the Seder is to provide a frame for remembering the Exodus, not only by liturgical recitation of the written texts of the

Haggadah, but also and above all by improvised "conversational remembering." Frames, as Erving Goffman has shown, organize our everyday life.[24] Thus, they relieve us from reflection and enable spontaneous action. With the Seder, we move on to the level of non-everyday behavior. This shift from an everyday frame to a festive and exceptional one is explicitly marked and foregrounded in the Haggadah, the script for the feast. The arrangements have to be so exceptional that they strike the minds of the uninitiated, and the youngest child has to ask the question that will trigger the chain of explanations and commemorations: "Why is this night so different from all other nights?"[25] This question addresses precisely the point of framing; it is the question of somebody who lacks the cue: "What is going on here?" The Seder starts with a festive enactment of a frame-shift.

"Difference" is a key word in the Seder ceremony. God is praised for having made a difference: between this night and all other nights, "between the sacred and the profane, between light and darkness, between Shabbat and the other six days of the week, and between Jews and Gentiles"—and between serfdom *(avodah)* and freedom *(kherût)*, which is the basic theme of the story to be remembered. All these differences are to be made understandable and palpable through the one difference which is sensually staged and brought to the forefront by the striking exceptionality and unfamiliarity of the arrangements and actions, of "what is going on." The children, the uninitiated, are provoked to ask, and the answers given serve the function of an initiation, of conveying and acquiring a new identity. This connection between question, answer, and identity is made clear by the "Midrash of the four sons."[26] At several places in the Torah, the answer is prescribed for when your son asks you about the meaning of the Law or one particular law. These passages are collected in this Midrash and attributed to four types of sons: the wise one, the wicked one, the simpleton, and the one who does not know how to ask.

> The wise one—what does he say? "What are the testimonies, and the statutes, and the laws that the LORD our God commanded you?" (Deut. 6:20). So you tell him about the laws of Pesach, that one may not eat anything whatsoever after the Pesach sacrifice.
> The wicked one—what does he say? "What is this service to you?" (Exodus 12:26). "To you," and not to him. And since he excluded himself from the people at large, he denies the foundation of our faith. So you

blunt his teeth and tell him, "It is because of this that the LORD acted for me when I came forth out of Egypt" (Exodus 13:8). "For me," and not for him; had he been there, he would not have been redeemed.

The simple son—what does he say? "What is this?" (Exodus 13:14). Tell him, "With a strong hand God took us out from Egypt, from the house of slavery" (Exodus 13:14).

As for the one who does not know how to ask, you must begin for him, as it is written: "And thou shalt tell thy son in that day, saying: It is because of this that the LORD acted for me when I came forth out of Egypt" (Exodus 13:8).

The Midrash of the four sons is a mini-drama about memory, history, and identity. The identity question is expressed by the play with the personal pronouns: I and me, us and our, you and he. The entire ceremony is about telling the story. This is history as it is remembered and told, not as it might have happened. The Seder provides a frame for telling and explaining the story. The important questions to ask are pretty much the same as those codified in the Latin hexameter quoted above:

Quís, quid, ubí, quibus aúxiliís, cur, quómodo, quándo?
Who?, what?, where?, by what means?, why?, how? and when?

Who tells the story? The father and the adult participants, who play the role of the emigrants from Egypt. To whom? To the children, who have to learn to identify with the group of the liberated slaves and to say "we" and "us" with respect to the ancient story. Why? Because this is the story that tells us who we are. When? On the occasion of the annual return of the time when this event is believed to have happened, the spring time of the offering of the first fruits. By which means, in which form? In the form of a 'symposium' (the Haggadah prescribes or recommends eating and drinking in "reclining posture," i.e., in Greek and Roman style[27]), and in a combination of liturgical and conversational remembering.

Trauma and triumph go together in liturgical memory. The triumph culminates in the crossing of the Red Sea where the persecuting Egyptians are drowned. This is the decisive act of liberation. The keyword is *bᵉ-yad khasaqah*, 'with strong arm.' Again and again this formula recurs in the liturgy, and its theological meaning is to represent the liberation as God's—and not Moses's—work, as a sign of God's power.[28] Even the recital of the ten plagues forms part of the Seder liturgy, spilling some drops of wine with every mention of a plague:

blood *(dam)*
frogs *(tzefarde')*
lice *(khinim)*
insects *('arov)*
pestilence *(däbär)*
boils *(sh'chîz)*
hail *(barad)*
locusts *(arbäh)*
darkness *(choscheq)*
killing the first-born *(makhat b'khorot)*[29]

The motif of the ten plagues elaborates the aspect of triumph, corresponding to the aspect of trauma by which both the Biblical book and the Seder Haggadah begin: the genocidal suffering of the Israelites under Pharaoh. It is interesting to note that the ten plagues, this strangest element of the Exodus narrative, play such an important role in the later adaptations and retellings of the story, starting with Psalms 78 and 105 that reduce the number to 7 (which is also the number of the plagues that are prophesied in the revelation of St. John, a passage clearly following the model of Exodus) and ending with Handel's oratorio *Israel in Egypt*, whose Parts II and III dwell on the theme of the plagues.

Liturgical memory—in the same way as cultural memory—provides a society with a connective structure working in both the social and the temporal dimensions. In the social dimension, it works as a social cement binding human beings to fellow human beings, creating a common space of experience, expectation, and action that provides trust, confidence, and orientation. In the temporal dimension, cultural connectivity works as a principle of continuity linking past, present, and future, in that it creates meaning, memory, and expectation by integrating the images and stories of the past into a continuous present. This aspect is the basis of myths and historical narratives such as the Exodus from Egypt. Both aspects, the normative/social and the narrative/temporal one, the aspect of instruction and the aspect of narration, consolidate belonging or identity, enable an individual to say "we."

In the Seder feast, however, the past is not only remembered but performed. The celebration does not scrupulously follow a fixed model, a ritual prescription, but it re-presents or 'presentifies,' in the sense of 'making present,' by a form of actual reliving. The recitation of the Haggadah is complemented by all kinds of improvised contributions about "our" sufferings in Egypt and the delights of liberation.

The themes of promise and future are also very prominent in the Seder liturgy, which closes with the proclamation *le shanah-haba'ah be-Yerushalayyim*, "Next year in Jerusalem!"—the expression of hope founded on memory.[30] Only he who remembers is able to look with confidence into the future.

Exodus and Utopia

This is the utopian aspect of Exodus. Like so many utopian texts, Exodus starts with a departure, with leaving home, setting out for an unknown goal in order to finally, and in most cases unexpectedly, arrive at an island where ideal conditions prevail. In Bacon's *Nova Atlantis*, which is typical of the genre in this respect, the newcomers have to undergo a moral transformation in order to be accepted into the new community and its ideal constitution and institutions. If we apply this pattern to Exodus, the parallels but also the differences become obvious. The departure is not for the absolutely unknown: there is a clearly indicated goal, first Mount Sinai and then Canaan. Nevertheless, there is a departure, there is an ideal constitution—to be received at Mount Sinai—and there is the land of milk and honey, a clear model of Cockaigne, the Schlaraffenland.[31] The book of Exodus, to be sure, is not meant as a utopia, such as Plato's *Nomoi*. The constitution as spelled out in the *sefer ha-b'rît* is to be real, and not ideal, is to be lived and not just aspired to. The Promised Land is not some fictional island of bliss but a very real geographic unit. Still, there is a utopian element in the myth of the Exodus that is responsible for its extraordinary radiance and vitality within and outside of Judaism.

The Puritans in the early seventeenth century, the time when Francis Bacon wrote *Nova Atlantis*, crossed the Atlantic Ocean and set out for America as a new Promised Land, identifying with the children of Israel going out of Egypt.[32] This was an act of memory as much as it was a revolutionary step forward into something new: a new society, a new constitution, a new attempt at becoming the people of God and performing the covenant as laid down in the Bible. The same may be said of the Puritan revolution, the civil wars, and Oliver Cromwell's protectorate from 1642 to 1659.[33] Similarly the Boers, emigrating from Holland in the seventeenth through the nineteenth centuries, identified with the Israelites, took South Africa as a New Canaan, and derived from their role as Chosen People the right to subjugate the indigenous population.

The myth, idea, or symbol of Exodus has two utopian aspects: political and theological. The political aspect stresses the promise of milk and honey in the Promised Land. The fulfillment of this promise requires resolution, courage, and trust in the help of God in taking the land into possession and subduing its inhabitants. The religious aspect stresses the promise of a union, a kind of cohabitation with God, who plans to dwell in the midst of his people. Here, the fulfillment requires conversion, the radical abdication of former and foreign religious beliefs and practices that are now denounced as heathenism and heresy and the iconoclastic destruction of visual forms of the divine, making room for the categorically invisible God who, in spite of his absolute transcendence (in the sense of non-immanence), insists on his presence in the midst of his people.

In its religious or theological aspect as a story of conversion, Exodus symbolizes the turn from polytheism to monotheism, and from primary religions, whose history stretches back to time immemorial, to secondary religions that were founded in historical time, supplanting, absorbing, and extinguishing everything that went before.[34] Exodus symbolizes the emancipation from a past that is viewed as worldliness, alienation from God, thoughtless immersion in unquestioned traditions. The Exodus of the children of Israel from Egypt stands for the emancipation of humanity from its embeddedness in the world and its political, natural, and cultural powers, and for the emancipation of the divine from mundane immanence.

Seen in this light, we realize that this exodus has never been fully completed. There have always been relapses, counter-movements in the direction not of freedom but of bondage. The memory of Egypt and of Pharaoh assumed ever new shapes and faces of oppression, persecution, and humiliation that made it necessary to renew the power and pathos of the Exodus in several waves of iconoclasm, emancipation, and even emigration, starting with the Reformation, especially in its extreme forms of Calvinism and Puritanism, and Enlightenment, especially in its pronounced anti-clericalism ("écrasez l'infâme"[35]). It was this undefeatable continuity of spiritual and political tyranny and oppression—sometimes latent, sometimes manifest—that kept the idea, the myth, the book, and the symbol of the Exodus alive.

3

FROM POLYTHEISM TO MONOTHEISM: EVOLUTION OR REVOLUTION?

Evolution in Nature and Culture

During the first millennium BCE there occurred a fundamental change in the ideas about the divine that we use to describe, in modern terminology, as a turn from polytheism to monotheism. This turn is commonly understood as a process of evolution. After all that we have learned about evolution, however, in the course of 2009, the "Darwin year," we are no longer able to use the term 'evolution' in such a naive and uninhibited way. Rather, we must carefully distinguish between natural and cultural evolution, or between a scientific and a humanistic concept of evolution.

The most important differences between natural and cultural evolution consist, I would argue, in two points: the mode of reproduction, and the question of visibility and observation. Natural evolution is based on the rhythm of sexual reproduction, that is, on the sequence of generations, which, depending on the species, may be a matter of days or of decades. Cultural evolution, on the other hand, is based, to use a term introduced by the late Jacques Derrida, on iteration and reiteration, the various ways in which cultural memory is produced, reproduced, circulated, and communicated.[1] The other point is even more important. Nature has neither memory nor any means of self-observation. Natural evolution, therefore, is not aiming at any goal; it does not imply any teleology, any logic of optimization. This is one of the most important lessons of the Darwin year.[2]

Culture, on the other hand, has both memory and means of self-observation. Besides invisible changes, there is always also consciously planned development. We may here distinguish among three modes of alteration: change, development, and evolution. "Change" is undirected alteration, such as is traditionally lamented, even in ancient Egypt, as *mutabilitas mundi.* In the sublunar world, nothing stays the same. Things are inexorably changing. Gardens grow wild, rivers change their course, prices rise and fall, edifices are raised and decay, languages and customs change, and whoever aspires to constancy and permanence must actively oppose this gravitation toward alteration.

Our notion of development, on the other hand, refers to a completely different kind of alteration. By the term 'development,' we understand a goal-directed alteration that follows an inner law or program, an 'entelechy,' to use Aristotle's term. Development aims at maturation, perfection, but also at decay and death. Development may be finite, but evolution never is. Evolution, applied to culture, transcends development in two ways: it refers to something much more complex and encompassing than a finite unit that changes according to an inner program; and it implies—unlike natural evolution, which is blind—an idea of gradation, optimization, and progress that is alien to natural evolution. This is because culture proceeds with open eyes; unlike nature, it has organs of self-observation at its disposal.

Thus we are dealing, with regard to culture, with at least three different kinds of alteration: change, development, and (cultural) evolution. Change excludes planning, in the same way as natural evolution excludes breeding. Development refers to finite units such as institutions, towns and cities, arts and technologies, even states and empires that may rise and fall. Evolution refers to units whose size or complexity transcends planning, such as religion, civility, mentality, and culture or civilization itself. On the level of culture, unlike that of nature, the notion of evolution may be confronted with an opposite term: that of revolution.

In opposition to evolution, revolution does not imply development but rupture, departure, and turning back. This is impossible in nature because it presupposes critical self-observation. In the light of this distinction, let us now examine how the path from polytheism to monotheism should be understood: as evolution or revolution. At first sight, nothing seems more natural than to interpret this change as an evolution from lower to higher ideas about the divine. This may, however, be a question of perspective. Humans tend to view their present situation as the apex of a climactic development and the highest step in the order of being. It is thus only natural that Christianity appears to Christians, and Islam to Muslims, as the highest form of religion. In the perspective of cultural studies, however, it is, first of all, important to free oneself from this cultural bias. In cultural studies, a certain form of methodical relativism is indispensable and unavoidable. This distinguishes them from normative disciplines such as theology, law, and philosophy. In this broad and irreducibly relativist approach, cultural studies only carry out their task as organs of cultural self-observation. Self-observation necessarily implies the ability to see oneself with the eyes of others.

A first step in this direction consists in historicizing the concept of religious evolution itself. Where does it come from; in what context did it emerge? My impression is that the idea of religious evolution, in the sense of progress from lower to higher ideas of the divine and forms of worship, is deeply rooted in monotheism itself. There is arguably no other religious tradition that is so deeply informed by this idea, an idea which monotheism probably first brought into the world. I would like to support this statement by means of three ancient concepts that are typical of the Jewish and Christian traditions. These are the ideas of *historia sacra*, of graded revelation or accommodation theory, and of a spiritualization of religion or, in the words of Sigmund Freud, of a progress in spirituality/intellectuality.

In Judaism, the concepts of religious and political development are inextricably interwoven and together form what in Christian traditions has been called *historia sacra* since Augustine and 'salvation history' since the nineteenth century. *Historia sacra* is the history of God and his Chosen People, and this history is seen in terms of progress from low to high and from suffering to redemption, at whose end stands the messianic time, eternal peace, or even the end of this world and the world to come.

In the Torah or Pentateuch, we find a clear distinction of three historical epochs: primal history from creation to Noah, which is a universal history concerning all mankind; a history of the patriarchs from Abraham until Joseph, which is the history of a family; and, after an interval of 430 years, the sojourn in Egypt—the history of Exodus, Sinai, and conquest, which is the history of a people. Sacred history proper begins with Abraham. Abraham is commissioned by God to leave Mesopotamia, where his father worked as a maker of idols. Abraham's emigration from Mesopotamia amounts, therefore, to an exodus from idolatry or polytheism to purer forms of worship. God formed a covenant with Abraham and promised to make him the ancestor of a great people and to make his progeny as numerous as the stars in heaven. This is already an instance of that evolutionary perspective which remains central in Judaism. This miraculous demographic multiplication occurred in Egypt, but the Hebrews were only transformed into a veritable people or nation when God liberated them through Moses from their Egyptian bondage and formed a new covenant based on detailed legislation. With this event started a new age. The time *ante legem* was over and the era *sub lege* began. Religion, which until Jacob had been a matter of intimate communication between God and the patriarchs, became institutionalized, with priesthood, festivals, ritual and purity laws, and rules of all kind. The Jews are still living in this second era of sacred history; the Christians, however, count a new age from the birth of Christ, the era *sub gratia*, under grace. Thus, it seems to me very plausible that evolutionism, with its belief in progress, is particularly rooted in Christian tradition.[3]

This Christian origin of the idea of evolution may also account for the fact that most theories of cultural evolution posit three steps, which seem to refer to the three stages *ante legem, sub lege*, and *sub gratia*. In the twelfth century, the monk Joachim a Flores connected these three stages with the Holy Trinity. Leaving the time *ante legem* aside, he associated the age *sub lege* with the Father, the age *sub gratia* with the Son, and the age to come, which he saw already dawning, with the Holy Spirit.[4] Secular theories of cultural evolution, in particular, tend to proceed in three steps. In the eighteenth century, Adam Ferguson divided cultural development into the three stages of "savagery," "barbarism," and "civilization," and this division was followed in the nineteenth century by the very influential anthropologist Lewis Henry Morgan. Marx and Engels turned this scheme into the triad of tribal, enslaving, and capitalist societies, promoting like Joachim a Flores a new age to come, the class-free society as the secular form of the messianic age. Also triadic are the famous model of Auguste Comte with its sequence of religion, metaphysics, and positivist science, and Edward Tylor's theory of religious evolution in the stages of animism, polytheism, and monotheism. All of these and many more, especially Hegel's philosophy of history, may be interpreted as secularized forms of sacred history.[5]

Like the concept of sacred history, the concept of graded revelation or divine accommodation implies God as an agent of change, and may in various regards be interpreted as a variant of the sacred history model. The model of graded revelation seems to be of Christian origin, because Christianity as a new sectarian movement saw itself confronted with a particular need for legitimation vis-à-vis the older Jewish tradition.[6] This was only possible by privileging the new over against the old and presenting the new as the true tradition: *verus* versus *vetus* Israel. Thus, the idea emerged of a truth that did not exist at the beginning but breaks through only in later stages of revelation. The law was only a preliminary and preparatory step, meant to educate mankind, as Saint Paul said, in preparation for Christ. In this context, early Christian theology developed many evolutionist concepts presenting Christianity as the goal of a universal human development. Some examples are Eusebius's concept of *praeparatio evangelica*, according to which all religions converge toward Christianity; Origen's idea of an *educatio generis humani*, which Lessing took up in the eighteenth century; and, most typical and widespread of all, the theory of accommodation. The argument for the latter runs like this: God adapted his revelation to the mental capacities of humankind, whose development was conceived of in terms of ontogeny. The age *ante legem* corresponds to childhood, when a human being must not yet be expected to observe strict norms. The age *sub lege* corresponds to adolescence, when a youth, by contrast, needs such norms. The age *sub gratia*, finally, corresponds to adulthood, when a mature being may decide for him- or herself, following his or her inner voice.

Thus, God in his mercy and condescension *(synkatabasis)* adapted to the intellectual level of developing mankind and waited until the time of the Roman Empire to exchange the law, the exterior norm, for faith, the inner certainty.

Unlike the two models of religious evolution mentioned so far, which are important only for the origin of the concept but not for its actuality, the third one is still valid and plays an important role in theories of religious evolution. This is the model of spiritualization or ethicalization of religion. This model is also the oldest one of the three, occurring already with the early Israelite prophets (Amos, Isaiah, Micah, and others), who criticize the sacrificial cult and insist on God's preference for justice and mercy. Widows and orphans are more important to God than incense and sheep. They thus insist on a change which they interpret as progress to a higher form of worship in the sense of an assimilation to God's will and nature. Since God is just and spiritual, progress means spiritualization and ethicalization. "You shall be holy for I am holy" is the motto, and the highest commandment in this context is the commandment to love one's neighbor. Sigmund Freud described monotheism in these terms; he understood Judaism as progress in spirituality/intellectuality *(Geistigkeit)*, using this classical Christian motif of distinguishing itself from Judaism in order to distinguish Judaism from paganism.[7] During the nineteenth century this parameter of religious evolution was fully adopted by the history and philosophy of religion, as, for example, in Max Weber's concepts of rationalization and disenchantment of the world.

The critique of the prophets, however, does not concern foreign religion but the Israelite religion itself. Nevertheless, there are quite a few polemical and satirical statements against pagan, especially Canaanite, religion as well, addressing topics such as magic, witchcraft, divination, necromancy, sacred prostitution, and, above all, human sacrifice, especially the sacrifice of the firstborn. In these polemical passages it becomes clear that Israelite monotheism already had to cope with problems similar to those encountered later by Christianity: the problems of a religion trying to replace older traditions with something new, and forced to legitimize the new as progress. Since religion is normally about permanence and the exclusion of change, the argumentative expenditure of legitimizing the new over against the old is particularly high. This may possibly be the origin of theology.

For us who have lived for millennia in the frame of these forms of theological legitimation, the reasons for preferring monotheism to paganism seem so self-evident that we tend to overlook their theological tendentiousness. Of course, the transition from paganism to monotheism has to be seen as progress. Who wants human sacrifices or witchcraft back? Nothing seems more natural than interpreting the change from human to animal sacrifice, such as the replacement of the offering of the firstborn son (Isaac) with a ram, as a veritable evolutionary achievement, in the same way as, later, animal sacrifice was replaced with the singing of hymns and prayers, or nonviolent rites such as the Eucharist. Without any doubt, we are dealing here with a genuine upward development, a progress in spirituality. With all these concepts, however, we are still moving within the internal framework of monotheist apologetics. There is no ritual evolutionism. Rites legitimize themselves through their unfathomable age but not through progressive humaneness.

From Monolatry to Monotheism

Yet the transition from polytheism to monotheism is certainly not a matter of *ritual* but of *ideas* about the divine. The question, thus, should be whether there is a change that might be interpreted as an evolution of *ideas*.[8] I would like to approach this question in the second part of this chapter by means of two phenomena. The first one concerns the transition from monolatry to monotheism in the Hebrew Bible—that is, from a position that recognizes the existence other gods but requires that only one be worshiped, to a position that denies the existence of other gods altogether.

The first position (monolatry) is most clearly expressed by the first commandment, an absolute key text as far as the question of god and gods, unity and plurality, is concerned.

> I am the LORD your God, who brought you out of the land of Egypt,
> out of the house of slavery. You shall have no other gods before me.

God does not say, "I am the Only one, there are no other gods except me." He does not present himself as the only creator of the universe, but as the liberator of Israel. He does not refer to the other gods as nonexistent, but as forbidden. They do not exist *for you* and in my sight. They have no business in the temple of the Lord.

As a matter of fact, the existence of other gods is not only not denied, but is even presupposed. What God demands of his people is loyalty and fidelity, exclusive faithfulness to one god which does not allow for any relations with other gods. If there were no other gods, the request for faithfulness would be meaningless. The basic metaphor is conjugal fidelity, God being the bridegroom and Israel the bride.[9] The other gods appear in the role of seducers wanting to lure Israel away from the way of God and because of whom Israel is constantly scolded by the prophets for fornicating with them.

Another image for the relationship between God and Israel is the political alliance.[10] In this case, too, it is strictly forbidden to serve two overlords at a time and, for example, to form an alliance with both the Assyrians and the Egyptians. If Israel were to form an alliance with the Egyptians, this would be regarded by the Assyrians as a *casus belli* and a reason for most cruel punishment. Unlike courtship and matrimony, the political alliance is no metaphor but the real thing, the model which is at the base of this completely novel form of religion. The covenant between God and Israel is a formal treaty or contract after the model of Hittite and Assyrian treaties with other states and vassals. God chooses tiny Israel from the plethora of peoples and leaves the other people to the other gods.

Israel chooses from the plethora of gods the god Yahweh, who delivered it from Egyptian bondage, and abstains from worshiping other gods. God among the gods, Israel among the peoples—this is the foundation on which this alliance or covenant is formed and sacred history proceeds.

One text in particular may stand, *pars pro toto*, for a great many similar statements in the Torah, the prophets, the psalms, and other Biblical books to characterize the position of monolatry that rests on the principle of loyalty and faithfulness. This position is typical of a certain textual layer in the Hebrew Bible that is most clearly represented by the book of Deuteronomy. Deuteronomy must date back, at least in its original form, to the seventh century BCE, for it uses the terminology and the imagery of the Assyrian vassal treaties, which it transposes or relocates to the relationship between god and people.[11]

Together with other texts informed by the same spirit, it has contributed to the survival of the Jewish people after the destruction of the temple, the collapse of the state, and the deportation of the elite to Babylon—a singular achievement that amounts to a miracle under the circumstances of the time. This miracle, in turn, helped this position, which before the exile had been only a minority movement, to win general acceptance and to become the mainstream course in Judaism and radical Protestantism to this day.

If we look around at the historical context, we may ascertain two counter-positions. One is the majority or mainstream position against which the Deuteronomist movement is fighting, at first as a minority and later as a victorious position.[12] The other is to be recognized in a position that we would classify as properly monotheistic, according to which there are no other gods, and consequently the other religions are worshiping not gods but fictions, idols, false fabrications of their own fantasy and craftsmanship.

We get to see the first position only in the polemical illumination of the Deuteronomist writings. We are obviously dealing here with a moderate and syncretistic polytheism: moderate, because there are only a few (instead of innumerable) deities involved, and syncretistic, because these deities are originally Canaanite, such as Baal and Ashera-Astarte. We are obviously to imagine their relationship in the form of a small pantheon presided over by Yahweh in the role of *summus deus*. The transition from this form of religion, which according to the books of Kings and Chronicles must have prevailed in the pre-exile kingdom until Josiah, to the

Deuteronomist position can in no way be understood as an evolutionary development. Rather, we are dealing here with a revolution that even involved bloodshed and massacres, if we may believe the Biblical record: Elijah massacring the priests of Baal, Jehu massacring the house of Ahab, and the atrocities accompanying Josiah's cult reform. All this certainly belongs more within the realm of fictional literature than of objective historiography. It is, however, highly significant that this transition is represented or remembered by the Biblical sources and in the perspective of the Deuteronomist position in such antagonistic terms, as a forced mass conversion as it were.

Particularly if and because these events are not historical facts but to be understood only symbolically, they are all the more significant and shed light on the forms in which the Israelites or Jews themselves remembered and valued this transition. There is no question of evolution.

With the other position of strict monotheism, the situation is different. We find this position in the texts of the later prophets, especially with Deutero-Isaiah. There we read in chapter 45:5–7:

> I am the LORD, and there is no other; there is no God besides Me. I will gird you, though you have not known Me, that they may know from the rising of the sun to its setting that there is none besides Me. I am the LORD, and there is no other; I form the light and create darkness, I make peace and create calamity; I, the LORD, do all these things.

Here, finally, God appears as universal creator:

> For thus says the LORD, Who created the heavens, Who is God, Who formed the earth and made it, Who has established it, Who did not create it in vain, Who formed it to be inhabited: "I am the LORD, and there is no other." (45:18)

Here, God changed from "the Lord who delivered thee from Egyptian bondage" to the "creator of heaven and earth" besides whom there is no other god. This change may very well be understood as a development from the incipient and immature to a mature and final stage, and as an evolution from lower to higher levels of imagining God. The Yahweh of the Deuteronomist Exodus tradition is a tribal or national god who forms an alliance with Israel; he represents himself as the god of the fathers and the liberator from Egyptian bondage, but not as the only and all-competent creator of the universe. Deutero-Isaiah's Yahweh, on the other hand, is a universal deity. Here, we may speak of an evolution of ideas, in the sense of an amplification of perspective, from ethnicity to universality or, in the words of Benjamin Nelson, from tribal brotherhood to universal otherhood.[13] We encounter this all-encompassing creator god also elsewhere in the Bible, for example, right at the beginning of Genesis.

We are dealing here, however, with an evolution, not from polytheism to monotheism but within monotheism, from monolatry to pure monotheism. Between poly- and monotheism, there is, in the Bible, no development, but only radical aversion and reversal. No way leads from one position to the other, but only a radical, revolutionary turn.

Egypt and Religious Change

In the last part of this chapter I would like to turn to Egypt. There is no more suitable example for our topic. Egypt confronts us with an unbelievable wealth of sources that in most cases are well determined in terms of chronology and provenance and that belong to a relatively limited timespan, the four centuries from 1500 to 1100 BCE. This time produced thousands of hymns primarily to the sun god, of which hundreds are preserved.[14] Within this corpus, a change is clearly discernible that may be interpreted as an evolution of ideas. There are, of course, very many texts that are older and younger than this time window. But there is not much change. The decisive transformation takes place during these centuries around 1300 BCE. In chapter 1, this discourse was presented as an example of 'explicit theology' that gained an unusual prominence in Egypt during the New Kingdom. Here, I would like to come back to these texts to ask in what sense they indicate a process of religious evolution or revolution. What is unique with this epoch is that it confronts us with both forms of a monotheistic turn: an evolutionary and a revolutionary one. For Egypt, this is a veritable "Axial Age."

We may divide this time period into sections of unequal length. The first section comprises the years from around 1500 until 1350, the second contains the twenty years from 1350 until 1330, and the third the time from 1330 until 1100. The dominating theological concept during the first period may be summarized under the concept of a 'theology of primacy.' This is a polytheism with a strong sense of unity. Everything is oriented toward one single god from whom all things originated or "emanated":

heaven and earth, humans and gods, animals and plants. God appears here absolutely as the universal creator, but 'creator' here means 'origin,' and the world that originated from God is a world to which the other gods also belong. By creating this world full of gods and other beings, God renounced his original uniqueness and became a god among gods, albeit the highest one among them. This theology of primacy is as old as pharaonic civilization, reaching back far before 1500 BCE. Characteristic of this theology is the combination and identification of three forms of relation: to originate from, to depend on, and to rule over. What emerges from an origin remains dependent on this origin. The Egyptians believed that all life evolves from the sun, which generates light and warmth by its radiation and time by its movement. Everything that originates from and through the sun remains dependent on the sun; without the sun there would be no life on earth. Up to this point we ourselves would still subscribe to this view.

The next step, however, is not so easy for us to take. 'To be dependent on' means, in Egyptian thinking, 'to be governed or ruled by.' The sun rules as lord or king over the world. It emits not only light and time, but also dominion. We must not forget that the Egyptians founded the first large territorial state in human history, and the theology of primacy dates back to the origin of this state, around 3000 BCE.

Around 1500, however, there starts to emerge a universalist perspective in addition to the traditional perspective of unity. Until that point, people were living in a world whose limits coincided with the borders of Egypt. The outside realm was not considered to be part of creation but of chaos. From 1500 onward the Egyptians started to have experiences that required a radically different outlook. In consequence of radical political changes which cannot be dealt with here—foreign dominion, the Hyksos, and wars of liberation—Egypt entered a network of political interconnections and became a global player among, beside, and above other powers of equal or lesser importance. These political changes caused a transformation of the traditional worldview. Egypt was no longer seen as coextensive with creation in the sense of an ordered world surrounded by chaos, but merely part of a far more comprehensive world containing many comparable nations and civilizations.

Humankind was now divided into four races: Egyptians, Libyans, Nubians, and Asiatics, or even five with the addition of the Minoans, Mycenaeans, and Aegeans, and the Egyptians believed the sun god and creator to be responsible for all of them. A hymn to the sun god, dating from the time of the liberation wars, praises him as

Atum, creator of human beings
who differentiates them and makes them live,
who distinguishes people by the color of their skin.[15]

This does not refer to differences among individuals but between races, languages, and forms of life.

When the primeval god, from whom everything originated, transformed himself into the sun and creator, he entered a boat, together with other deities, in order to circle around the earth by day and by night, above and below, and by these means to animate, organize, and preserve his creation. This concept, the most central and important idea of the ancient Egyptian world image, underwent a decisive transformation that begins to be evident in the texts around 1400. The distance between the sun god and the other gods grows larger and larger until eventually he circles the world alone in his barque. Although the other gods still exist as creatures of the sun god along with humans, animals, and plants, the monotheistic perspective now becomes much more dominant.

This new world image became radicalized by Akhenaten, who ascended to the throne of Egypt around 1350 BCE: the other gods were abolished, their temples closed, their priests fired, their images destroyed, their names erased, their cults and feasts discontinued. On the one hand, these actions may be regarded as the apex of a development that began two hundred years earlier; on the other hand, this is clearly a violent act that must be interpreted in terms of revolution rather than evolution.

For Akhenaten, there exists only one god: the sun. However, the sun no longer crosses the sky and the netherworld in a boat, but is stripped of all anthropomorphic traits and represented as a disk or globe with rays ending in hands (this being the only remaining anthropomorphism). In Akhenaten's hymns the universalist perspective reaches its height.

You made the earth following your heart when you were alone,
With people, herds, and flocks;
All upon earth that walks on legs,
All on high that fly on wings,

The foreign lands of Syria and Nubia,
The land of Egypt.
You set every man in his place, you supply their needs;
Everyone has his food, his lifetime is counted.

Their tongues differ in speech,
Their characters likewise;
Their skins are distinct, for you distinguished the people.

You made Hapy in the netherworld,
You bring him when you will,
To nourish the people, for you made them for yourself.
Lord of all, who toils for them,
Lord of all lands who shines for them,
Sun disk of daytime, great in glory!

All distant lands, you keep them alive:
You made a heavenly Nile descend for them;
He makes waves on the mountains like the sea,
To drench their fields with what they need.

How efficient are your plans, O Lord of eternity!
A Hapy from heaven for foreign peoples
And for the creatures in the desert that walk on legs,
But for Egypt the Hapy who comes from the netherworld.[16]

The monotheism of Akhenaten is no less consequential and radical than the position of Deutero-Isaiah eight hundred years later. For Akhenaten, as for Deutero-Isaiah, there is only one God. In two of his hymns we read: "You one and only God besides whom there is no other god."[17] The god of Akhenaten, however, is the sun and only the sun. His theology is not anthropomorphic but heliomorphic, and more of a cosmology than a theology. Akhenaten drew new and revolutionary conclusions from the traditional idea that the sun generates not only light and warmth through its radiation but also time through its motion. If the whole of reality derives from light and time, the other gods are superfluous fictions without any part in the creation and preservation of the universe. Their cults must be discontinued, their temples closed, their images destroyed, their names erased, their priests dismissed, and their feasts abolished.

Unlike the monotheism of Deutero-Isaiah, however, the monotheism of Akhenaten remained a short episode in Egypt. After the death of the king, the old gods were reintroduced and every trace of the new religion and its founder erased. Surprisingly enough, however, the evolution of ideas that culminated in Akhenaten's revolution was by no means arrested, let alone reversed. On the contrary, the priests of Thebes responded to Akhenaten's attack by developing—as shown in chapter 1 in somewhat greater detail—a new theo-cosmology based on a new theological category: the *ba* concept.

The *ba* concept denotes an immaterial vital force that animates the body in life and separates itself from the body in death. The theologians adopted this concept for redefining the relation between God and the world, a world that was again seen as being inhabited by gods and humans. Now, the highest god, the origin of all, is conceived of as a *ba* incorporated into the world like the human *ba* in a human body. At the same time, the many gods who keep the world going may be referred to as the many *ba*s of the transcendent One, in the sense of being his immanent manifestations.

In what sense might this innovation be understood as a step in an evolutionary process, a step forward? With the *ba* concept, a completely new form had been discovered to conceive of the relation between unity and diversity in terms of transcendence and immanence.

The old paradigm of primacy and creation is now not superseded but complemented by the new paradigm of transcendence and manifestation. In the framework of the first paradigm, that of creation and primacy, the divine as unity was conceivable only in terms of preexistence, as prior and exterior to the created world. The relation between God and world thus became temporalized: God as One before the cosmogony, God among many within the world. Now, a category was found by means of the *ba* concept to conceive of God as unity together with or simultaneous to the created world. The idea of God as origin and creator before the world was now complemented by God as transcendent power that manifests and hides itself in the world. This God does not confront the world from outside, but penetrates and animates it from within, and at the same time exceeds it.

This change from a polytheism of primacy with a strong perspective of unity to a kind of inclusive monotheism that views the many gods as manifestations of the Hidden One confronts us with a veritable evolution of ideas. There is no antagonism, no rejection of tradition involved, but a process that may be understood in terms of an evolutionary logic. This is confirmed by the fact that the same process may be observed with other religions. Referring to Indian religion, the medievalist C.S. Lewis once wrote:

> Monotheism should not be regarded as the rival of polytheism, but rather as its maturity. Where you find polytheism, combined with any speculative power and any leisure for speculation, monotheism will sooner or later arise as a natural development. The principle, I understand, is well illustrated in the history of Indian religion. Behind the gods arises the One, and the gods as well as the men are only his dreams. That is one way of disposing of the many . . . the gods are to be aspects, manifestations, temporary or partial embodiments of the single power.[18]

Yet there is, of course, also the other monotheism, the monotheism of Akhenaten and Moses that does not allow for other gods. This monotheism is by no means the maturity of polytheism but its opposite and its declared enemy. We must therefore distinguish between two forms of monotheism: inclusive monotheism, which can be understood as the maturity of polytheism because it is implicit right from the beginning as a perspective of unity, and exclusive monotheism, which is reached only by resolute reversion or conversion. In the same way, we are dealing with two dynamics of change in the history of religion: the dynamics of revolution and the dynamics of evolution.

We have identified the dynamics of evolution as an evolution of ideas. This is a very special phenomenon requiring many conditions to come about, and a quasi-natural process. An evolution of ideas requires especially the following four conditions: writing, discourse, a certain degree of professionalization, and the rise of lay theology. Writing makes it possible for former positions to remain present and accessible for later reference. Discourse means that such reference takes place and the debate is continued across generations. Professionalization means that specialists are exempt from manual labor and educated for taking up the debate, and lay theology means that the debate on religious ideas spreads beyond the circles of professional priesthood and is taken up by media of wider circulation. Under these circumstances, even religion, which normally strives to exclude change and sticks to the ancient and sacred traditions, comes under the influence of new concepts and cultural trends. Religion, it is true, has its true center and foundation in cult, but it transcends cult by reflecting on the conditions of cultic communication and the nature of the divine, and in these "trans-cultic" concerns, an evolution of ideas may become possible.

With regard to religion, an evolution of ideas is called 'theology.' Theology flourished especially in the context of those religions that arose from revolutionary impulses, such as Judaism, Christianity, and Islam, where there was an urge to legitimate the new truth and to defend it against regressive paganism and heresies. Under these pressures, all three monotheistic religions developed theologies, professional discourses on the nature of the divine that were codified in written form so that later positions could build on former ones. In Egypt, theology became possible because from the early fifteenth century BCE onward the Egyptian priesthood, at least the more important clergies, started to be based on a professional structure, and because the theological discourse unfolded in written form, in hundreds of inscriptions and papyri. Here the discourse arose from problems such as how to account for the existence of suffering and destruction in a world created by a benevolent and all-providing deity, and how to conceive of the relationship between the one and the many, God and gods, God and the world.

To come back to the question that was our point of departure: is the transition from polytheism to monotheism to be explained in terms of evolution?

The answer is "yes," if we understand by monotheism inclusive monotheism in the sense of C.S. Lewis, following the principle "All gods are One." The answer is "no," if we are dealing with exclusive monotheism following the principle "No god but God." This position is reached not by slow development and maturation, as it were, but by radical rejection and aversion. Here, the old is not absorbed into the new, but is the object of persecution, abomination, repression, and annihilation. Therefore, we should conceive of the religious transformations in the ancient world as fueled by two dynamics, an evolutionary and a revolutionary one: the evolutionary aiming at ever more adequate and in this sense "truer" representations of the divine, and the revolutionary one breaking with tradition in acts of creative destruction and seeking truth in other directions. Both impulses may be active within one and the same religion. We have to learn to account for both. We must avoid rejecting the other religions as disbelief, paganism, or heresy, and yet must be conscious of what we deem incompatible with our own ideas about the divine.

4

MOSES AND AKHENATEN:
MEMORY AND HISTORY

Moses and Akhenaten

Akhenaten is a figure of history without memory; Moses is a figure of memory without history. The two thus complement each other perfectly and are often associated, even identified, in modern literature. A figure of memory—what does this mean? What I mean by this formula is a person, historical or fictional, who lives in tradition, in myths, legends, pictures, works of history or fiction, whose sayings are quoted, whose tomb, if known, is visited, who may even receive a kind of cult. Moses is such a figure. He does not receive a cult and his tomb is not known, but in any other respect he is enormously alive in all kinds of cultural and religious traditions. Nothing of that kind exists for Akhenaten. More or less immediately after his death, he was subjected to a complete *damnatio memoriae*, his monuments destroyed, his buildings dismantled, his name erased from the lists of kings. On the other hand, he is a figure of history, all the more so as there is no non-historical tradition that could have transformed and distorted his image. No doubt about his historical existence is possible. Born around 1360 BCE—the dates are not absolutely sure—he ascended to the throne around 1345 and reigned for seventeen years, the first six years at Thebes, the following years at his newly built capital Akhetaten, the modern Tell al-Amarna. He was married to Nefertiti, with whom he had six daughters, and from another wife he had a son, Tutankhamun, who reigned after him and returned to Thebes or Memphis and to the old religion. Archaeology has been able to unearth a wealth of art, architecture, and textual evidence, so that Akhenaten's time is now the best-known episode in Egyptian history. Nothing of this sort exists for Moses. There are no contemporary documents, Egyptian or Hebrew, mentioning his name;

61

it is even completely unclear what 'contemporary' could mean in this respect. We cannot be sure whether and at what time Moses ever lived.

The forgotten pharaoh: Stages of his discovery

1714	Pater Sicard's sketches of boundary stelae
1824	Wilkinson discovers the rock tombs
1828	Champollion's brief visit to Amarna
1843/45	Lepsius spends ten days at Amarna
1851	Lepsius publishes his interpretation of Amenophis IV/Akhenaten as "founder of a pure solar cult"
1883/84	Bouriant copies the most important religious inscriptions, among them the "Great Hymn to the Aten"
1895	Breasted writes his Berlin dissertation "De Hymnis in Solem sub Rege Amenophide IV conceptis," comparing the Great Hymn and Psalm 104
1906	Breasted, in his History of Egypt, describes Akhenaten's religion as a precursor of Biblical monotheism

The rediscovery of Akhenaten during the second half of the nine-teenth century ranks among the most important achievements of Egyptology. The history of archaeology is full of sensational discoveries, but none is more exciting or inspires more debate in the intellectual world than the rediscovery of Akhenaten and his reign. What archaeology brought to light was not only a city with temples, palaces, villas, houses, sculptures, texts, and the like, but a religious revolution of immense consequences: the abolition of traditional religion and the institution of a new and apparently monotheistic cult, the first founding of a religion in history. It is true that this new foundation remained an episode of no more than twenty years, but it meant a deep and far-reaching change in Egyptian culture and religion. It is hardly imaginable that such an event would not have left any traces in the collective memory of the people, which must have been deeply affected by the destruction of its religious traditions.

From the beginning of the eighteenth century, several travelers visited the ruins of Tell al-Amarna, but the credit for the rediscovery is due to Carl Richard Lepsius, the founding father of German Egyptology, who visited Amarna in 1845 and six years later presented the forgotten pharaoh in a memoir as the successor to Amenophis III and "a bold reformer" who "attempted nothing less than a purification . . . of the entire Egyptian national religion, by radically reducing the religious traditions to their origin, the cult of the sun, and admitting the disk as its sole image."[1] Forty-four years later, the young American Egyptologist James Henry Breasted revealed in his Berlin dissertation striking parallels between the Great Hymn of Akhenaten and Psalm 104. No Egyptian hymn outside Amarna—of which there are hundreds, even thousands, preserved—comes as close to this text as the Hebrew psalm! In 1910, the British Egyptologist Arthur Weigall published a rather romantic biography of Akhenaten that made Akhenaten the most popular figure of ancient Egyptian history. Within little more than half a century, Akhenaten came to be seen as the first monotheist, the first individual, the precursor of Moses.

One of the most attentive observers of these discoveries was Sigmund Freud, who as early as 1910 recommended Akhenaten to his disciple Karl Abraham as a topic for historical psychoanalysis. Abraham's study appeared in 1911. Sixty years had sufficed to provide the rediscovered pharaoh with a mythical aura that by far eclipsed every other figure of Egyptian history.

Freud himself returned to Akhenaten and Moses only twenty-three years later, when in 1934, under the pressure of anti-Semitic persecution, he started working on his last book, *Moses and Monotheism*.[2] In this book, he is not interested in an individual psychoanalysis of Akhenaten but in a collective psychoanalysis of the Jewish people. "In view of the new persecutions," he wrote to Lou Andreas Salome and Arnold Zweig, "one wonders again how the Jew came to be what he is and why he attracted this undying hatred," and the answer he found was "Moses hat den Juden geschaffen," "Moses created the Jewish character."[3] With breathtaking boldness, Freud postulated that Moses was an Egyptian, a follower of Akhenaten and his new solar monotheism, who organized the Exodus from Egypt in order to rescue the new religion from being extinguished in Egypt. The first and strongest argument for Moses's Egyptian nationality is his name, which is undoubtedly Egyptian, meaning 'born of,' like the Greek ending '-genes.' Thutmose corresponds to Hermogenes, Ramose to Heliogenes, Amenmose to Diogenes, and so on. In a Jewish context, the theophoric element had to be dropped, of course. Even more interesting than its Egyptian etymology is the fact that the Hebrew text is unaware of it and supplies a Hebrew etymology that does not work, deriving the name Moshe from Hebrew *mashah*, 'to draw'; but *moshe*, then, would mean 'the one who draws,' not 'the drawn one.' The Hebrew text thus reveals itself to be ambiguous and to cover a hidden truth.

In a similar vein, Freud reads the story of Moses's birth as the inverted mythical scheme of the birth of the hero, from riches to rags, so to speak, from an Egyptian prince to a Hebrew slave, and explains this inversion as an attempt at "judaizing" an Egyptian hero. He also considers the assonance of "Aten" and "Adonai," but fortunately does not pursue this idea any further. Strangely enough, the parallels between the Great Hymn and Psalm 104[4] seem to have escaped him. Among his most ingenious observations, however, is his explanation of Moses's "heavy tongue": according to Freud, this motif refers to Moses's poor command of the Hebrew language, for which reason he needed Aaron as an interpreter. All this is not completely impossible, it is only impossible to prove.

What, in Freud's eyes, did Moses and Akhenaten have in common to bring them into such a close relationship, to make Moses an Egyptian and to derive Biblical monotheism from Egyptian Atenism? Freud saw the common elements of the two religions in the following five points:

both proclaim a strict monotheism, showing the most intransigent
    intolerance against traditional polytheism;
both exclude magical rites and ceremonies;
both are aniconic;
both stress ethical requirements; and
both discard any concept of a hereafter and of human immortality.

Today, one would perhaps agree with points one and three, but certainly not with two, four, and five. It is true that in the Amarna religion there is hardly any magic and very little ritual, whereas in the Mosaic religion there is a plethora of rites. The stress on ethics in the Mosaic religion is obvious, but in Amarna, the ethical aspect of God is absent in the most striking manner. In Amarna, the traditional concept of a hereafter is discarded, replaced by a new one according to which the human person lives on in the form of his *ba*, leaving the tomb during the day and entering it at night. Above all, however, Akhenaten's god is the sun and nothing but the sun, whereas the god of Moses is the liberator from Egyptian bondage, an actor in history. In fact, the two religions are worlds apart. However, points one and three, exclusive monotheism and iconoclasm, were felt to be strong enough to associate Moses and Akhenaten, not only by Freud and many others in the wake of the rediscovery of Akhenaten and his religion in the twentieth century, but already, as will be shown later on, in antiquity.

Freud's boldest thesis, however, is still to follow. According to Freud, Moses was eventually killed by the Hebrews, who were no longer able to bear with his abstract and demanding monotheism. In this, Freud was following Ernst Sellin, an Old Testament scholar. In his book *Mose und seine Bedeutung für die israelitisch-jüdische Religionsgeschichte* (Moses and His Importance for the History of Israelite-Jewish Religion),[5] Sellin proposed a solution for the enigma of the servant of God in Isaiah 53, identifying the suffering servant with Moses.[6] Isaiah 53 thus not only provided the model for narrating the story of the crucifixion of Christ but was in itself, according to this doubtlessly ingenious interpretation, a symbolic articulation of the memory of Moses.[7] Sellin later abandoned his thesis concerning the real killing of Moses, for the wish to kill him is sufficient for turning him into a martyr of God, but Freud obstinately stuck to his idea of the murder of Moses because he needed the fact for his psychoanalysis of Judaism. According to his theory, the murder of Moses was a reenactment of the primal parricide.

It would be worthwhile to understand how it was that the monotheist idea made such a deep impression precisely on the Jewish people and that they were able to maintain it so tenaciously. It is possible, I think, to find an answer. Fate had brought the great deed and misdeed of primeval days, the killing of the father, closer to the Jewish people by causing them to repeat it on the person of Moses, an outstanding father figure. It was a case of "acting out" instead of remembering, as happens so often with neurotics during the work of analysis.[8]

Reenactment—instead of remembering—led to a retraumatization which, in turn, caused suppression and latency, according to the typical progress of a neurotic illness: "Early trauma—defence—latency—outbreak of neurotic illness—partial return of the repressed. Such is the formula which we have laid down for the development of the neurosis."[9] Freud transposes this formula from the individual to the collective level and now feels able to explain the six centuries between Moses—a contemporary of Akhenaten, thus living in the fourteenth century—and the appearance of the prophets at the end of the eighth century as a period of latency. With this explanation, he thinks he has found the solution to another enigma: how was it possible that a demanding and unpopular religion such as monotheism could ever have made its way with such irresistible force? It was a case of the return of the repressed:

> A tradition that was based only on communication could not lead to the compulsive character that attaches to religious phenomena. It would be listened to, judged, and perhaps dismissed, like any other piece of information from outside, it would never attain the privilege of being liberated from the constraint of logical thought. It must have undergone the fate of being repressed, the condition of lingering in the unconscious, before it is able to display such powerful effects on its return, to bring the masses under its spell.[10]

Freud had been criticized, especially by Yosef Hayim Yerushalmi, for his concepts of phylogenetic memory and unconscious transmission.[11] How could the memory of an experience such as the primal parricide and its reenactment through the murder of Moses be biologically, genetically transmitted? Freud's argument was that neurotic children show in their reactions to early traumas a behavior toward their parents that seems "unjustified in the individual case and only becomes intelligible phylogenically—by their connection with the experience of earlier generations."[12] And he continues: "If we assume the survival of these memory traces in the archaic heritage we have bridged the gulf between individual and group psychology: we can deal with peoples as we do with the individual neurotic."[13] Yerushalmi characterizes this theory as "Lamarckism," because Lamarck had postulated the heredity of acquired characteristics. This is correct, of course, but Freud's question is not, in the first place, how these memories could have been transmitted, but how the memory of Moses and his monotheism could have met with such an enormous resonance eight hundred years after the hypothetical lifetime of Moses.

It is a theory of trauma or, in the terminology of Aleida Assmann, of "impact and resonance."[14] Some unprecedented and incomprehensively overwhelming "impact event" creates a kind of resonance in such a form that later events are experienced as a return of the original event. This, however, is not a matter of centuries but of generations.

Yet the whole problem of latency and transmission arises only if we believe in the historicity of Moses and his having lived in the time of Akhenaten. It vanishes if we assume that the whole mythology about

Moses, Exodus, Sinai, wilderness, and conquest is a creation of the seventh and sixth centuries, with some beginnings in the eighth century, and building on older traditions about the Hyksos, their sojourn in and expulsion from Egypt, the Egyptian occupation of Canaan, and Hebrew or 'Apiru resistance. There is, then, no gap between Moses and Deuteronomy. The historical events between, say, 730 and 530 BCE become all the more important, with the fall of the Northern Kingdom in 722 as the traumatizing "impact event" and the fall of Jerusalem in 587 as the decisive retraumatization.

What we may thus retain from Freud's reconstruction of the origin and victory of monotheism is the element of trauma and resonance. We should, however, replace Freud's concepts of the traumatic event—the primal parricide and its reenactment through the murder of Moses—with the historical events, the catastrophe first of the Northern, then of the Southern kingdoms, and his concepts of phylogenic memory and genetic transmission with the concept of resonance, a psychic disposition shaped and reinforced by historical experiences.

Akhenaten

Let us now turn to Akhenaten and the religious revolution associated with his name. The idea of making the sun god the only god is not completely out of tune with religious tradition in Egypt. Implicit in Egyptian polytheism was what could be called a 'cosmogonic monotheism.' Everything existing, including the gods, has one origin: it originated from the sun god, who is the only uncreated being: Kheper-djesef, 'who came into being by himself,' *autogenes* in Greek, *causa sui* in Latin. The universe evolved out of the first sunrise, when the sun god changed from unconscious, inert preexistence in the primeval waters to conscious, creative existence. Thus there has always been in Egyptian religion a very strong monistic perspective, of one god from whom the whole universe emerged, and who does not confront the universe from without, like the Biblical creator, but who animates it from within. Cosmogonic monotheism sees the world not so much as creation but rather as emanation, but the two concepts do not exclude each other in Egyptian thought; they are constantly mentioned together as two complementary models. The world is seen both as a creation and as a transformation of god.

This monistic perspective grows stronger and stronger during the New Kingdom. A generation before Akhenaten, there are already hymns describing the daily course of the sun no longer as a collective enterprise involving all the other gods, but as a solitary action of the sun god, who now actually confronts the world from without or above. Yet the world is still full of gods. Akhenaten simply did away with these other gods because he felt that the whole of reality could be explained as the work of the sun god alone, who creates the visible reality by his light, warmth, and radiation, and who generates time through his motion. If the gods are unnecessary to explain reality, they are fictitious and must be abandoned. Akhenaten's revolution is but a radicalization of tendencies that became increasingly perceptible in the course of the Eighteenth Dynasty.[15]

What seems to me most important about this radicalization is its more scientific than religious character. Behind this revolution was not a religious revelation, but a cosmological discovery: the universal dependency of everything existing on the sun, on light, and on time. Akhenaten's abolition of traditional religion was an act of radical enlightenment, rather than the installation of a new religion.[16]

The rejection of other gods is the sole element that the two monotheisms, Akhenaten's and Moses's, have in common. In all other respects, they are worlds apart. In Egypt, the abolition of traditional polytheism by Akhenaten was the consequence of a cosmological revolution. Akhenaten discovered that light and time were sufficient to explain the whole of reality.[17] The other gods had no share in this and had to be discarded as false and nonexistent. In Israel, the rejection of other gods was a matter of faith and loyalty that had nothing to do with cosmology. On the contrary, the existence of other gods was not denied. Loyalty to the one, to Yahweh alone, was the motto, and loyalty only makes sense if there are other gods to lure one into disloyalty. In the context of the Exodus tradition, Yahweh was worshiped, not as the sole creator of heaven and earth, but as the liberator from Egyptian bondage. The difference between Akhenaten and Moses could not be greater. The basic idea behind Akhenaten's reform was the cosmological theory of the sun as the origin and sustainer of everything existing. The basic idea behind Moses's institution was the political concept of the covenant between Yahweh and Israel, for which the Assyrian vassal treaties and loyalty oaths were adopted as a model.[18] As far as history is concerned, there is no connection between Amarna and Israel or Akhenaten and Moses. The situation changes, however, when we turn from history to mnemohistory, the history of memory.

The Egyptian Trauma

It is easily imaginable, and considerable evidence points to the fact, that for the majority of Egyptians, the age of Amarna was one of destruction, persecution, suppression, and godlessness—of "darkness by day," the formula used to refer to the experience of divine absence.[19] The gods had turned away from Egypt.

The experience of being forsaken by the gods as a result of a heinous crime, unspeakable in the truest sense of the word, found apparent confirmation in the severe crises that beset Egypt toward the end of the age of Amarna, among them a plague, the "Canaanite illness."[20] The Restoration Stela of Tutankhamun refers to this desolation:

> The temples were desolated,
> their holy places were on the verge of disintegration,
> they had become piles of rubble,
> overgrown with thistles.
> Their chapels were as if they had never been,
> their temple precincts were trodden roads.
> The land was in grave ailment,
> the gods had turned their backs on this land.
> If one sent soldiers to Syria
> to extend the frontiers of Egypt,
> they had no success.
> If one appealed to a god for succor,
> he did not come.
> If one besought a goddess, likewise,
> she came not.
> Their hearts had grown weak in their bodies,
> for "they" had destroyed what had been created.[21]

This text has the advantage of being a contemporary testimony. It employs the term 'trauma'; the Egyptian expression 'grave ailment' (*zeni-menet*) comes as close to 'trauma' as possible. It is a quotation from a famous text, the "Prophecies of Neferti," where this expression is used to describe the inversion of social order.

> I show you the land in grave ailment:
> The weak is strong,

One salutes him who saluted,
I show you the uppermost undermost,
What has turned on the back turns on the belly.
Men will live in the graveyard,
The beggar will gain riches,
The great will rob to live.[22]

Tutankhamun takes this expression, applies it to the Amarna experience, and gives it a religious meaning. There are very few royal inscriptions that deal with traumatic experiences and times of intense suffering. In this respect, the stela of Tutankhamun is exceptional and highly important.

The most important evidence for the traumatic character of the Amarna experience, however, is to be found in Egyptian sources only about a thousand years later. In this case, we are fully justified in speaking of repression, latency, and the return of the repressed. However, I would prefer to interpret this case as well in the light of Aleida Assmann's theory of "impact and resonance."[23] The notion of 'resonance' refers to the human inclination to comprehend new experiences in the light of past experiences serving as model or schema. In this way, traditional Judaism used to term historical catastrophes *hurbân*, a term that originally designated the destruction of the Second Temple.[24] The term 'impact,' by contrast, refers to events that exceed all traditional models and schemata and produce speechlessness. Such an event was the one that later came to be called *shoah*, or 'holocaust.' Maybe the Amarna experience was the same kind of impact event for the Egyptians, becoming accessible to verbal articulation only much later. This happened, in fact, six hundred years later in a historical situation that had many things in common with the historical context in which the Exodus narrative emerged. Some vague memory traces of Amarna must have survived in Egyptian oral tradition. What reactivated these traces was the experience of four devastating Assyrian invasions in the first half of the seventh century that not only destroyed the Egyptian temples and hijacked the cult images, but also forced Egypt into vassaldom. This overwhelmingly traumatic experience provided a frame of coherence and meaning for older memories of comparable character: of the Hyksos invasion and domination in the seventeenth and sixteenth centuries and the Amarna experience that, in the light of the Assyrian trauma, appeared also as a kind of invasion, albeit an invasion from within. This frame is a typical phenomenon of resonance. Egyptian history now came to be seen as characterized by three severe traumas and their triumphant reversals: the Hyksos domination, the Amarna revolution, and the Assyrian invasions. This late Egyptian view of Egyptian history found its expression above all in three traditions: (1) the legend of the lepers; (2) an apocryphal interpretation of the three great pyramids; and (3) a new mythology around the god Seth, who now came to incorporate the image of the foreign invader who enters Egypt from the north, destroys the temples, and reveals the mysteries, until Horus from the south succeeds in pushing him back and expelling him from Egypt. This mythology is acted out in all temples in a number of rituals and in the main festival of the temple of Edfu.

The Legend of the Lepers

I am referring to the famous story that Flavius Josephus excerpted from Manetho's lost Egyptian history. This is the text that, more than two thousand years before Freud, brings Akhenaten and Moses together, as we shall see, and even identifies the two. Manetho, an Egyptian priest, wrote his book by royal commission in the first quarter of the third century BCE. Josephus inserted his more or less faithful copy into his pamphlet *Contra Apionem* about 350 years later.[25] In this story there appears a certain priest Osarseph, who made himself the leader of a colony of lepers. After having given his colony laws that overturned Egyptian customs—not to worship any god, not to spare any sacred animal, not to mix with outsiders—he assumed the name Moyses. He then formed an alliance with the Hyksos, who had been expelled from Egypt two hundred years earlier. They settled in Jerusalem, conquered Egypt, and tyrannized the country in the most terrible way, destroying the temples and cult images and roasting the sacred animals in fire. After thirteen years of suffering, however, the exiled king was able to return and to expel the usurper and the invaders.

Until recently, Flavius Josephus's readers saw in this story a version of the Exodus, because they were unable to understand the information Manetho gives about its location in Egyptian history. The story mentions a king Amenophis who "wants to see the god" and, writes Manetho, "communicated his desire to his namesake Amenophis son of Paapios, who, in virtue of his wisdom and knowledge of the future, was reputed to be a partaker of divine nature. This namesake, then, replied that he would be able to see the gods if he cleansed the whole land of lepers and other polluted persons."[26] Since this Amenophis son of Hapu is a well-known historical person, living under Amenophis III, the king can be no other than Amenophis III, the father of Akhenaten.[27] This and other details, such as the thirteen years of oppression, point to the Amarna experience as the historical background of the story. Hence Manetho's Osarseph is but a place-holder for Akhenaten, whose name was removed from the king lists, and who is thus already in this text associated and even identified with Moses. Moreover, Manetho distinguishes carefully between this and the Hyksos trauma, writing that the lepers and their allies "treated the people so impiously and savagely that the domination of the Hyksos seemed like a golden age to those who witnessed the present enormities."[28] He then continues with a graphic description of these enormities and concludes: "It is said that the priest who framed their constitution and their laws was a native of Heliopolis named Osarseph after the god Osiris, worshipped at Heliopolis; but when he joined this people, he changed his name and was called Moses."[29]

There are many variants of this story in Hellenistic Egyptian historiography, all of them carefully collected by Flavius Josephus in his book *Contra Apionem*, Apion being one among them. In these more summary versions, most of the details that refer to the Amarna trauma are lost, and it is the Exodus reference that prevails. The existence of so many different versions points to the fact that we are dealing here with oral tradition. Josephus himself remarks that Manetho did not draw the story "*ek ton ieron grammaton*"—'from the sacred writings'—but reports "*mytheuomena kai legomena*" ('myths and legends').[30]

In this early case, it is obvious what prompted the equation. The common elements here are the prohibition of worshiping the gods and iconoclasm, the prohibition and destruction of images. Manetho's or Josephus's text brings together a memory of the Amarna episode and an anti-Semitic cliché, interpreting Judaism as atheism.

The Reinterpretation of the Pyramids

The interpretation of Manetho's story as a distorted memory of the Amarna experience, which was first proposed in 1904 by the historian Eduard Meyer,[31] no longer needs a lengthy demonstration. It is now almost universally accepted. The most interesting aspect of this representation of Akhenaten and his time is that it shows this episode of Egyptian history in the light of a national trauma. When, almost thirty years ago, I pointed to the dark side of the Amarna experience—and I think I was the first to do so—writing of brutal persecution, intolerance, police control, I had no idea of this tradition, which I discovered for myself only ten years later.[32] Since the concept of 'trauma' had not been introduced into historical discourse then, I called it a "culture shock," meaning, however, what now has come to be generally called trauma.

Because of its traumatic character, the Amarna episode did not, despite the complete destruction of traces and *damnatio memoriae*, vanish altogether from collective memory but survived, in however distorted a form.[33] The testimony of the Manetho story is corroborated by a passage in Diodorus's book on Egypt whose true significance has only recently been discovered by the Danish Egyptologist Kim Ryholt.[34] In chapter 64 of the first book of his *Bibliotheca historica*, Diodorus speaks of the three great pyramids and reports two different traditions about their builders. The first, and correct, one ascribes them to Khufu (Cheops), Khafre (Chephren), and Menkaure (Mycerinus). But there is also another one, ascribing them to Armaios, Amasis, and Inaros. Nobody has ever been able to make sense of this strange remark, but Ryholt's explanation is absolutely convincing. Armaios is Horemheb, who put an end to the Amarna revolt and was the first king to continue the king list after it broke off after Amenophis III; Amasis is Ahmose, the victor against the Hyksos invaders who ruled Egypt for over a hundred years; and Inaros is a hero who fought against the Assyrians. The three pyramids appear, in this interpretation, as three monuments of trauma and triumph: the Hyksos trauma and its ending by Ahmose-Amasis is commemorated by the Khafre pyramid, the Amarna trauma and its ending by Horemheb-Armaios is commemorated by the Khufu pyramid, the greatest of the three, and the trauma that the four Assyrian invasions wrought upon Egypt is commemorated by the Menkaure pyramid, which is ascribed to Inaros I, the hero of several stories of Egyptian resistance. Kings Amenophis III and Bocchoris, who ruled Egypt before the Amarna episode and the Assyrian invasions, also appear in stories where a time of suffering is prophesied, such as the "Oracle of the Potter" and the "Oracle of the Lamb." Also the Osarseph story is dated by Manetho explicitly in the time of Amenophis III. Thus there cannot be any doubt that in ancient Egyptian collective history there existed a tradition about three traumatic experiences, historical catastrophes, and their triumphant reversal: the Hyksos domination in the seventeenth and sixteenth centuries, the Amarna revolution in the fourteenth century, and the Assyrian invasions in the seventh century BCE.

It is more than probable that this tradition originated in the seventh century under the weight of Assyrian domination that must have been felt—in the same way as in Israel—as a time of severe suffering. In this time, one might assume, older memories and traditions about Amarna and the Hyksos were reactivated. It was, however, the Amarna memory that gave these national traumas the character of a religious crime, its character of iconoclasm and "theoclasm," creating what could be identified as the central late Egyptian phobia: that the various mysteries of the religious centers in Egypt would be exposed, the cult images would be destroyed, the sacred animals would be slaughtered, and the gods would separate themselves from Egypt—*dolenda secessio*, as the "Asclepius Apocalypse" has it.[35]

The Late Egyptian myth of the god Seth as an invader, conquering Egypt from the north (as did the Hyksos and the Assyrians, and later the Persians, the Greeks, and the Romans), destroying the temples, revealing the mysteries, and arresting the sun in its course, but eventually to be repelled from the south by the victorious Horus, becomes the central national narrative that gives expression to these fears. In a ritual to be performed in the temples of Egypt in order to ward off the invader, the sun god is appealed to, that he may intervene and stop Seth in his murderous attack.

Behold, Seth, the rebel, has come on his way,
he has turned once more to Egypt,
to plunder with his hand.
He is in the course of appropriating the land by force,
in accordance with the way he behaved before
when he destroyed the holy sites,
when he tore down their chapels,
when he made uproar in the temples.
He has inflicted suffering, he has repeated injury,
he has made unrest rise up anew.
He has brought suffering to the sanctuary,
he has planned rebellion in Memphis.
Behold, he penetrates into the Serapeum,
he has brought injury to the house of Opet.[36]

The lament of this ritual recitation strongly resembles the description of Egyptian suffering and lamenting in the "Oracle of the Lamb":

Woe upon Egypt! [It weeps] for the manifold curses that will befall it.
Heliopolis weeps because the East has become too [. . .]
Bubastis weeps. Nilopolis weeps,
because the streets of Sebennytos have been made into a vineyard
and because the mooring post of Mendes has become a bundle of palm
  leaves and persea twigs.
The great priests of Upoke weep.
Memphis weeps, the city of Apis.
Thebes weeps, the city of Amun.
Letopolis weeps, the city of Shu.
Fear conceives suffering.[37]

These facts shed an entirely new light both on the character of the
Amarna episode as a period of suffering, as it must have been experienced by the greater part of the Egyptian people and as it must have
lived on in the collective memory, and on the late Egyptian mentality as one informed by strong resonances of traumatic experiences and
haunted by phobic fears of their return. However, these connections
also shed a new light on the reasons why Manetho or a later redactor
could identify his Osarseph, the 'screen memory' or mask of the suppressed Akhenaten, with Moses, and why Josephus, consequently, could
read the fantastic story of the lepers as a malicious rendering of the
Jewish Exodus tradition.

Exodus and Trauma
There are several striking parallels between the Egyptian trauma tradition and the Biblical Exodus story which only now become visible. First:
the Exodus narrative also tells the story from trauma to triumph, from
severest suffering and oppression to liberation and autonomy (in this
case, theonomy). Second: this story also contains the motif of Egyptian
suffering in the form of the ten plagues. The Egyptian narrative of suffering at the hand of strangers or lepers and their eventual expulsion is here
integrated into the overarching Hebrew narrative of suppression and liberation. Hebrew suffering leads to Egyptian suffering. Egyptian suffering
leads to Hebrew liberation.

In Israel, the Exodus narrative arose around the same time and under
similar circumstances as did the narrative about the three traumas in
Egypt: in the time of the Assyrian, and later Babylonian, pressure and

conquest during the eighth through the sixth centuries. Israel and Egypt shared the general historical situation and came into even closer contact under Persian and Greek domination. In Palestine, there must have been legendary oral traditions about the Hyksos and their expulsion from Egypt, about the oppressive Egyptian occupation of the Levant in the Late Bronze Age, and the resistance movement of the 'Apiru, which could have galvanized under Assyrian pressure into the triumphant Exodus narrative, in the same way that in Egypt the legendary traditions about Amarna galvanized into the phobic legend of the lepers and the Egyptian versions of the Exodus story, as well as the mythology of the foreign invader and religious criminal.

We thus see that the Hebrew Exodus narrative and the Egyptian invader narrative—if we may subsume the three traditions of the story of the lepers, the legend about the pyramids, and the mythology of Seth under this term—correspond to each other in many respects. Both are national narratives, centered around a collective self-image, and both originated in the same historical context of the Assyrian crisis. In other respects, these correspondences are to be viewed as inversions rather than parallels. Both are informed by a phobic vision, in the Egyptian case the fear of invasion, in the Hebrew case inversely the fear of dispersion as displayed in great and gruesome detail in Deuteronomy 28. The central fear in Egypt was the return of the religious destruction; the central fear in Israel was the loss of the Promised Land and the expulsion into diaspora. Both fears came true.

The decisive correspondence—in the sense of inversion—is, however, of a religious nature. The greatest abhorrence and anathema that the Assyrians inflicted upon the land of Israel was idolatry, the installation of idols in the temple at Jerusalem. For Egypt, the greatest horror was the destruction or abduction of the cult images. In the eyes of the Israelites, the erection of images meant the destruction of divine presence; in the eyes of the Egyptians, this same effect was attained by the destruction of images. In Egypt, iconoclasm was the most terrible religious crime; in Israel, it was idolatry. In this respect, Osarseph alias Akhenaten, the iconoclast, and the Golden Calf, the paragon of idolatry, correspond to each other inversely, and it is strange that Aaron could so easily avoid the role of the religious criminal. It is more than probable that these traditions evolved under mutual influence. In this respect, Moses and Akhenaten became, after all, closely related.

The promise that God gave to Moses and the Israelites was not restricted to the Promised Land that flows with milk and honey. There was another promise, and this was even more decisive: that God will dwell in the midst of His people.[38]

We must not forget that the books that tell the story of the Exodus and emphasize this promise form part of the "Priestly Code." For the priests, it is not the conquest of the Promised Land, but the community with God, that forms the highest goal to be achieved by the Exodus from Egypt. This cohabitation of God and men requires the "holiness" of the people—"You shall be holy as I am holy" (Leviticus 19:2)—implying the strict observance of the law and strict loyalty (no other gods), meaning the complete absence of "idols," whose presence in Israel would put an end to any community between God and his people.

Cohabitation with the divine was also the Egyptian ideal. The Amarna trauma was the experience that the gods had denounced this community and had retired, closing all communication with mankind. The "Asclepius Apocalypse," dating from the second or third century CE, stresses precisely this point: the cessation of human and divine cohabitation and communication. Chapter 24 is about the statues that ensure divine presence and that are animated by it. Chapter 25 continues with a description of what will happen to Egypt and the world when these images are destroyed and their cult discontinued.

And yet there will come a time when it will be seen that the piety and unremitting devotion with which the Egyptians have worshipped the gods was futile and that all sacred addresses to the gods will be vain and fruitless. For the deity will ascend once more from the earth to the heavens and forsake Egypt. This land, once the seat of religion, will then be bereft of divine presence. Foreigners will inhabit this land, and not only will the old cults be neglected, but religion, piety, and the cult of the gods will be actively prohibited by law. Of the Egyptian religion only fables will remain and inscribed stones. . . . In those days the people will be weary of life and will cease to revere and venerate the cosmos. This Whole, so good that there never was, is, nor will be anything better, will be in danger of disappearing for good, the people will regard it as a burden and revile it. They will no longer love this world, this incomparable work of God, this glorious edifice, fashioned from an infinite variety of forms, instrument of the divine will, pouring its favor unstintingly into its work, where in harmonious variety everything worthy of worship, praise, and love shows itself as One and All. Darkness will be preferred to light, death to life. No one will raise his eyes to heaven. The pious will be taken for madmen, the godless for wise, the evil for good. . . .

The gods will turn away from men—O painful separation!—and only the evil demons will remain, mingling with men and driving their wretched victims by force into all kinds of crime, into war, robbery, fraud, and everything hateful to the nature of the soul.

Then will the earth no longer be solid and the sea no longer navigable, the heavens will not hold the stars in their orbits, nor will the stars keep to their course in the firmament. Every divine voice will necessarily fall silent. The fruits of the earth will rot, the soil will become barren, the very air will be oppressive and heavy. And these things will hold sway in the senescent world: absence of religion, of order, and of understanding.[39]

5

ANCIENT EGYPT AND THE
THEORY OF THE AXIAL AGE

The Theory of the Axial Age

In a book written immediately after the end of the Second World War, entitled *Vom Ursprung und Ziel der Geschichte* ("On the Origin and Goal of History"), the philosopher Karl Jaspers identified the centuries around the middle of the first millennium BCE as the origin of the modern world and coined for this period of general transformation the term "the Axial Age."[1] By this term, Jaspers means the time when the first texts were written that we are still reading, when the first great individuals arose that we still admire, when the religions were founded that we still practice. In Jaspers's understanding, the Axial Age separates the premodern and the modern, and he postulates a principal similarity of all pre-axial civilizations sharing the features of pre-axiality, as well as a similarity of all axial civilizations sharing the features of axiality. Moreover, he declared a categorical difference between the pre-axial and the axial worlds, a difference so great, that is, that comparison between the two becomes meaningless. The more similarity there is among the axial civilizations, the less there is between the axial and the pre-axial worlds. The negation of similarity renders difference and comparison meaningless.

The Axial Age, in Jaspers's view, triggered an evolution of global significance. A realm of understanding emerged comprising different traditions, from China to the west, and three thousand years of history. On the other side of this evolution, the pre-axial world sank into the darkness of intellectual inaccessibility. Here lies the provocation, the challenge of Jaspers's theory for disciplines such as Egyptology that specialize in civilizations of the pre-axial and in this sense premodern world. Therefore, every attempt at understanding premodern phenomena such as ancient

Egyptian texts requires a deconstruction of this very high, very radical barrier between the axial and the non-axial. The approach to be taken here is somewhat reductionist: it is based on the evolution of writing. My idea is that this evolution did not proceed in only one decisive step, the invention of writing, dividing the history of a given culture into "before" and "after" in the same way as Jaspers's Axial Age, but in at least three steps of equal importance. In the light of this specific history, the transition from archaic to modern, from the pre-axial to the axial world, loses its radical character.

In Jaspers's view, this transition or transformation amounts to a quantum leap and a veritable mutation of the human race. In the centuries around 500 BCE, the Axial Age, Jaspers wrote, "man, as we know him today, came into being," *homo sapiens axialis*, so to speak. "The whole of humanity performed a leap."[2] "In this time period," he wrote, "the fundamental categories were created in the frame of which we are thinking until today, the world religions were founded, on which mankind lives until today."[3] This similarity in thought and experience that links our world to the Axial Age, and according to which modernity begins around 500 BCE, is the source of our ability to read and to enjoy texts dating as far back as the eighth century BCE, such as Homer or Isaiah, or that belong to cultures as distant as India and China. The Axial Age marks the boundary of our understanding. Within this cultural and temporal horizon of almost three thousand years, understanding is possible; to quote Jaspers again: "Der Ursprung des Verstehens ist unsere Gegenwärtigkeit, das Hier und Jetzt" ('The origin of understanding is our presence in the here and now').[4]

What distinguishes "pre-axial" texts from "axial" texts such as Isaiah and Homer? Jaspers and his followers say: their degree of reflexivity. But how can we be sure about the degree of reflexivity implicit in pre-axial texts? I would like to give a very different answer to the question about the distinction between axial and pre-axial texts. The reason that we can more or less easily identify with texts such as Isaiah and Homer is that they came down to us in an unbroken tradition of interpretation, whereas the Babylonian and Egyptian texts were only discovered and deciphered in the course of the last hundred to 150 years. The same applies to all the other "axial" texts. Their secret is canonization and interpretation. Jaspers knew, of course, that writing was invented around 3000 BCE in Mesopotamia and Egypt, thus much too early for his axial turn. This may be the reason why he totally neglected the media question. The Toronto school—Marshall McLuhan, Eric Havelock, and more recently Friedrich

Kittler—who put the media question right in the center of their theory of cultural development, took the invention of alphabetic writing to be the decisive step.[5] However, this excluded the east, whose integration into the axial transformation had been the whole point of the Axial Age theory since its first formulation by Abraham Hyacinthe Anquetil-Duperron (1731–1805), the discoverer of the Zend-Avesta. He identified a "grande révolution du genre humain" that occurred around the middle of the first millennium BCE all over the ancient world, from China to Greece.[6] Many Orientalists, among them the Sinologists Jean-Pierre Abel-Rémusat (1788–1832) and Victor von Strauss (1809–99), elaborated on this thesis during the nineteenth century until it came to the sociologist Alfred Weber in Heidelberg, from whom Jaspers took it over. These scholars held that around 500 BCE the first founded religions emerged, such as Biblical monotheism, Zoroastrianism, Buddhism, and Jainism, as well as the first philosophical and theoretical writings, in the west from the pre-Socratics to Aristotle, and in the east from Kautilya, Panini, and other Indian theorists to Confucius, Lao-tzu, Meng-tzu, and other Chinese philosophers. Jaspers's contribution, apart from introducing the term "Axial Age," consisted in the hermeneutical approach, in raising the question of understanding that concerns us here. If we want to keep this general idea, we cannot attribute the intellectual transformation of the ancient world merely to the invention of the Greek alphabet.

Writing as an Agent of Change

First of all, we must distinguish between *systems* and *cultures* of writing. Writing *systems* concern differences such as ideographic, logographic, syllabic, and alphabetic scripts. Writing *cultures* concern functions of writing and forms of its social embedding. The decisive steps in the evolution of writing are due less to changes of writing *system* than of writing *culture*.

All the major scripts that are currently in use stem from only two sources: the Chinese script, and the scripts of the ancient Near East such as Egyptian hieroglyphs and Sumerian cuneiform. This fact alone gives us an idea of the interconnectedness of cultural phenomena. The invention of writing is indeed an event of axial magnitude, dividing the world into literate and oral societies. But it was not the invention as such that led to axial transformations. This was only the first step, and I will try to show that it was a *third* step in the process of literacy that definitively changed the world.

Before going into these details concerning the evolution and impact of literacy, however, I would like to start with a remark of a more general character. Writing as a cultural technique may be viewed under two different aspects, one pointing to the future and the other to the past: as an *enabling* factor, making cultural creations possible which would otherwise never exist, and as a *preserving* factor, keeping things in memory and accessible to later retrieval that would otherwise vanish and be forgotten. Writing, in short, is a factor of cultural *creativity* bringing about change and innovation, and a factor of cultural *memory* keeping the past present and permitting recourse to earlier texts and ideas. It is an agent of both acceleration and retention, of change and of permanence and continuity. Until now, it has always been studied as a factor of progress and evolution, stressing its enabling aspect as a cultural technique. Let me illustrate this point by the example of musical notation.

There are still many traditions of music that are untouched by musical notation and that correspond to what in the domain of language is called orality. They differ mainly in two points from literate musical traditions: in standardization and innovation. 'Oral' musical traditions tend to be less standardized and less innovative. They are more complex in their use of features that cannot be rendered in musical notation and in spontaneous improvisation, and they are less complex and innovative in the lack of polyphony and a certain formulaic repetitiveness which is also characteristic of oral literature. The kind of music, however, that develops in the realm of writing shows a breathtaking speed and range of evolution; only consider what happened in the 250 years between Monteverdi and Verdi. This evolution is a matter both of creativity and of memory. Musical notation enables the composer to create music of unprecedented complexity, and it founds a memory that determines the directions of development by intertextual competition. The history of western music would not have been possible without the invention of musical notation. This invention brought about a truly axial turn in that it triggered an evolution of global significance. It put every form of music untouched by it into the position of 'folk' or 'ethnic' music, comparable to the position of oral societies outside of Jaspers's history.

What we may learn from this example about the impact of writing is that a pressure to innovate is created that is alien to the realm of orality. There is no more eloquent testimony for this pressure that the complaint of Khakheperreseneb, an ancient Egyptian author writing in the beginning of the second millennium BCE:

Had I but unknown phrases, strange expressions,
new speech that has not yet occurred, free of repetition,
no transmitted proverbs used by the ancestors!
I quench my body of all it contains
and relieve it from all my words.
For what has been said is repetition
and nothing is said that has not been said.
One cannot boast with the utterances of the ancestors
for posterity will find out.
O that I knew what others ignore
and what is not repetition![7]

This poignant complaint refers to a problem which only the author has. The public expects the familiar from the bard, but from the author something new. The author has to position himself in a space of intertextual competition. Khakheperreseneb's complaint contains many typically axial motifs such as reflexivity, interiority, individuality: "I quench my body."

Let us now turn to a more detailed analysis of the different steps in the evolution of writing culture (not writing systems). The first step, the invention of writing, led to what I propose to call 'sectorial literacy.'[8] In this stage, writing is used exclusively in those sectors of cultural activity for whose needs it had been invented. In the case of Mesopotamia, these are economy and administration. In Egypt, too, these are its central functions; besides these, however, writing is also used for political representation, funerary monuments, and cultic recitation.

In China, writing seems to have originated in the context of divination. In Minoan and Mycenean Greece, writing (Linear A and B) never transcended the realm of economy (bookkeeping) and vanished with the end of the economic system (the palace culture) that needed it. In Egypt, Mesopotamia, and China, however, the realm of writing soon expanded into other fields of cultural practice.

Literacy and Cultural Memory
The turn from 'sectorial' to 'cultural' literacy occurs when writing enters the central core of culture, which Aleida Assmann and I call 'cultural memory.'[9] What matters here is not whether we are dealing with an alphabet (either consonantic or vocalized), a syllabic, logographic, or ideographic script, but whether or not writing is used for

the composition, transmission, and circulation of 'cultural texts.' This is the second step toward axiality. It occurred in Mesopotamia toward the end of the third millennium BCE, when the sagas of the Gilgamesh cycle were first collected into a continuous epic, and in Egypt at the beginning of the second millennium BCE, where the first truly literary texts were composed.

Cultural memory is that form of collective memory that enables a society to transmit its central values and patterns of orientation to future generations and, by doing so, to continue its identity over the passing of time. Cultural memory provides a kind of connective structure in both the social and temporal dimensions. It provides that kind of knowledge which enables an individual to belong, and since human beings need to belong, they fulfill this need by acquiring the relevant knowledge, which in German is called *Bildung*, in Greek *paideia*, in Hebrew *musar*, and in Egyptian *sebayt*. With these concepts we associate institutions of reading and writing—libraries, schools, universities—and find it hard to imagine a kind of cultural memory that is not based on writing and literacy.

The contrary, however, is the case. Orality and ritual are the natural media of cultural memory, frequently accompanied by basic methods of notation or pre-writing such as the Australian *tjurunga*s, the knotted cords (*quipu*s) of the Incas, and the like. Most of the time, these oral mnemotechniques were found to be much more efficient than the early forms of writing. This has many reasons. First, the contents of cultural memory, such as the great narratives about the origin of the world, the tribe, and its central institutions, the moral norms, and similar cultural texts, are, so to speak, 'mnemophile'; they stick in the memory because of their poetic beauty and substantial relevance. We must not forget that writing was invented to record the non-mnemophile, the contingent data of economy and administration which no human memory can retain for long. Second, the various cultural texts (I am using this term in the sense of Clifford Geertz, who described the Balinese cock fight as a cultural text) tend to be multi-media, involving besides language pantomime, music, dance, and ritual, and may not be easily reduced to that one stratum of symbolic articulation that lends itself to transcription into writing. For this reason, it took the Mesopotamians and Egyptians more than a millennium to take this second step from sectorial to cultural literacy. When writing is introduced into this domain, however, there is a high degree of probability that it will lead to far-reaching transformations.

When writing enters the realm of cultural memory, there seem to be three options: either to transcribe the oral texts and transform them into literature, or to compose entirely new texts whose complexity requires writing for their initial conceptualization and composition, or, finally, a combination of both. Mesopotamia and Israel seem to belong to the third category, Greece to the first, and Egypt to the second. The Homeric epics present themselves as transcripts of an oral performance; they exhibit their oral character. The same holds for Greek lyrical poetry, drama, and even the Platonic dialogues. This is not to exclude the possibility that Homer used writing for the composition of his epics. I am only stressing the fact that they imitate the form of oral composition and presentation. In Egypt, the situation is different. The earliest literary texts, such as the "Instructions" of Ptahhotep and Amenemhat I, the "Instructions" for Merikare, the complaints of Ipuwer and Khakheperreseneb, the prophecies of Neferti, and the tales of the Shipwrecked Sailor, of Sinuhe, and of the Eloquent Peasant, exhibit their genuinely literary character in the richness of their vocabulary and grammar and in their structural complexity.[10] In Egypt, the use of writing for the work of cultural memory does not lead to the transcription or textualization of oral texts, but to the composition of new, genuinely written texts, much in the same way as the introduction of writing in western music culture led to the composition of a new kind of music, polyphony. Not until five hundred years later, in the New Kingdom and especially in the Ramesside Period (thirteenth century), was the use of writing extended to typically oral genres such as folk tales, love songs, harpers' songs, and so on. These disappeared again, however, from the realm of writing after 1100 BCE.

With the literarization of significant parts of cultural memory and the production of cultural texts that are *conceptually* literate (requiring writing for their initial composition and addressing a reader), a writing culture changes from sectorial to cultural literacy. In this stage, the techniques of writing and reading affect the connective structure of a society. One of the typical effects of this transformation is the construction of a glorious, heroic, or classical past or "antiquity."[11] The cultural memory becomes two-storied, divided into the new and the old, modernity and antiquity. An important factor in this development is linguistic change. The older texts within the literary tradition that now become validated as 'classics' preserve a linguistic stage that no longer corresponds to the spoken language of the present. At a certain time, this distance between the classical and the vernacular idiom grows so big that the classical language has to be learned specifically, and we are dealing with cultural diglossia. Cultural diglossia is reached where and when the other language characterizes the *cultural* texts, those texts that carry the normative and formative knowledge, which constitutes and transmits a cultural identity across the sequence of generations and forms the diachronic backbone or connective structure of a society. This stage of cultural evolution characterizes the Kassite age in Mesopotamia (1550–1150 BCE) and the Ramesside age in Egypt (1300–1100 BCE).

The construction of a classical, heroic, or "golden" age, an antiquity as a past to look back to for models of behavior and literary production, means a first step in the direction of canonization. This cultural split into antiquity and modernity seems to me to be one of the characteristic elements of axiality. It introduces into a given culture an element of critical distance and reflexivity.

At a certain stage, every literate culture enters the stage of a split culture, divided into the old and the new, and it is writing in the form of cultural literacy that brings this split about. Even the typically Egyptian association of this split with the idea of immortality may, at least to a certain degree, be generalized. In its literate, written form, cultural memory appears as a timeless or at least imperishable realm of immortality which one may enter by creating a book or work of art of everlasting beauty, truth, or significance. This idea of literary or artistic immortality may be considered a first step in the direction of transcendence or transcendental visions, which Shmuel Eisenstadt, in particular, stresses as a decisive factor of axiality. The use of writing for the fulfillment of the desire to transcend one's lifespan and to live on in the memory of posterity dates back, in Egypt, to the very beginnings of literate culture, but I would classify this use of writing for tomb inscriptions as sectorial literacy. The step toward cultural literacy is achieved when the tomb monument is topped by the literary work, for example in the words of Horace, who said with regard to his book of odes: *Exegi monumentum aere perennius / regalique situ pyramidum altius* ('I have created a monument more lasting than bronze / And higher than the royal site of the pyramids'). This motif appears already in an Egyptian text where it is said of the classical authors:

They have not created for themselves pyramids of bronze
nor stelae of iron;

they have not contrived to leave heirs in the form of children,
to keep their names alive.
But they created themselves books as heirs
and teachings that they have written.
They employed the scroll as lector priest
and the slate as "loving son."
Teachings are their pyramids,
the reed their son,
the polished stone surface their wife.
Their tomb chapels are forgotten,
but their names are recalled on their writings, that they have created,
as they endure by virtue of their perfection.
Their creators are remembered in eternity.[12]

We are not yet dealing here with "real" axiality because this step of canonization is still culture-specific and lacks the global claims typical of axial
movements. But it is a step in the direction of axiality, and it is a step
within the realm of written culture.

Another sphere of cultural memory which is strongly affected by the
use of writing is history. The existence of written sources about the past
draws the distinction not only between the old and the new, but between
myth and history. The use of written records creates history in the sense
of a critical discourse, separating mythical tales about the past from rea-
soned accounts of documented history. This step seems to be a Greek
achievement, but the Greeks themselves attributed it to the Egyptians,
opposing their own mythical form of historical consciousness to Egyptian
history, which is based on written records. Typical examples of this inter-
cultural comparison are Herodotus's account of Hecataeus's visit with the
priests of Amun at Thebes[13] and Plato's account of Solon's visit with the
priests at Sais.[14] Both Hecataeus and Solon confront the Egyptian priests
with Greek traditions about the past. Hecataeus recites his own geneal-
ogy, which leads, after fifteen generations, to a god as the ancestor of
the family, and Solon tells the Greek version of the story of the flood,
the myth about Deukalion and Pyrrha. Both are then confronted by the
Egyptians with their records. Hecataeus is led into the temple, where
he is shown 341 statues of high priests, one the son of the other and
no god interfering, documenting 11,340 years of purely human history.
Solon is shown the Egyptian annals stretching back over more than nine

thousand years, where the memory of Athens's glorious past is preserved, for example their victory over Atlantis, which in Greece itself has been destroyed and forgotten. All this is, of course, pure fabulation, but it illustrates the principle of critical history with its distinction between myth and history, brought about by the use of writing for chronological bookkeeping which, in the form of annals and king lists, belonged to the first and most important applications of writing in Egypt and Mesopotamia. In this sense of documented past and critical verifiability, it is writing that produced history and dispelled mythology. Writing caused history to be where myth was, because it documented conditions in which not gods but human kings reigned and humans were responsible for their actions. Writing bestows upon historical memory the quality of verifiability and adds a truth value to its accounts about the past which myth, in spite of its truth claims, is lacking.

A third domain of cultural memory where the use of writing leads to dramatic changes is religion. It is here that the second and decisive step toward canonization is achieved, a step of truly global significance, which, in my opinion, forms the very center of Jaspers's concept of the Axial Age. In the realm of religion, writing appears with the same critical pathos as in the sphere of history, opposing its superior truth to the invalidated truth claims of myth. Here, its claims to superior truth are based on revelation, which it codifies. All world religions—Judaism, Christianity, Islam, Buddhism, Jainism, Sikhism, Confucianism, Taoism—are founded on a canon of sacred scripture that codifies the will of their founder and the superior truth of his revelation. This step of canonization was invented only twice in the world: with the Hebrew and the Buddhist canons. All later canons followed these examples. This second step of canonization changed the world in a truly 'axial' way.[15]

Secondary Canonization and the Rise of Exegesis

The first step of canonization, which we encountered in Egypt and Mesopotamia, led to a cultural split into antiquity and modernity, drawing a distinction within the culture. Canonization here means the selection of the timelessly authoritative and exemplary from the plethora of written literature. The second step of canonization applies a different criterion: the criterion of absolute and universal truth, drawing a distinction that sets a new religion off against all other religions, including the culture's own past religions, which now become excluded as paganism, idolatry, heresy, and error. Some elements of this pathos of distinction and exclusion seem to me to be still present in Jaspers's concept of the Axial Age, which in this respect appears to me as a secularized version of the religious distinction between paganism and true religion. His idea of axial civilizations puts the pre- and extra-axial world in a position similar to the Jewish, Christian, and Islamic construction of paganism. This aspect becomes even stronger with Benjamin Schwartz's definition of the Axial Age as the "age of transcendence" and Shmuel Eisenstadt's concept of "transcendental visions" as the hallmark of axiality. All this is to a large degree a feat of cultural memory and an effect of writing and canonization. We know nothing about the transcendental visions of shamans, kings, priests, and seers unless they are not only written down but, above all, are received into a canon of sacred scripture. Only then do they become part of cultural memory and religious identity.

In the west, the Hebrew canon of sacred scripture is complemented by a Greek and Latin canon of classical literature. The cultural memory of the west rests on these two projects of canonization, which were conducted roughly simultaneously—and probably not entirely independently—by specialists in Palestine and Alexandria. The distinctive hallmark of what I call secondary canonization is *the rise of exegesis*. In the stage of primary canonization, the texts selected as classics exist in a form which the medievalist Paul Zumthor called "*mouvance*."[16] The texts were constantly reformulated, amplified, or substituted by other texts in order to accommodate them to the changing conditions of understanding. Their "surface structure" was sacrificed in order to save at least part of their meaning. This is why even written texts, over a long stretch of time, tend to exist in many different versions. The continuous growth of the book of Isaiah, first into Deutero-Isaiah, then into Trito-Isaiah, is a typical case of how a cultural text changes in what the Assyriologist Leo Oppenheim called "the stream of tradition."[17] The Epic of Gilgamesh developed in the course of its transmission and redaction from a cycle of sagas into the twelve-tablet composition that appears in the Neoassyrian library of Assurbanipal at Nineveh. In a similar way, the Egyptian *Book of the Dead* developed from just a pool of unconnected spells, out of which every individual funerary papyrus picked its own specific selection, into a real book with a fixed selection of 167 spells in a fixed order. Written texts, in this "stream of tradition," share to a certain degree the changing character of oral texts.

This flexibility, or *mouvance*, is categorically stopped and excluded by the process of secondary canonization.[18] Secondary canonization means the combination of a *sacralization of surface structure* (the prohibition of adding, changing, or subtracting a word) typical of sacred texts like hymns, incantations, and ritual spells on the one hand, and the *preservation of meaning* typical of cultural texts in the state of *mouvance* as the constant adaptation of the text to changing conditions of understanding on the other hand. Sacred texts are not necessarily cultural texts, since they may be known only to specialists and withheld from public circulation. Sacred texts are verbal enshrinements of the holy. In sacred texts, not a syllable must be changed in order to ensure the 'magical' power of the words to 'presentify' (or 'make present') the divine. In this context, it is not understanding that matters, but correctness of pronunciation, ritual purity of the speaker, and other requirements concerning proper circumstances of performance. As the case of the Rig Veda shows, this principle of non-*mouvance* and verbatim fixation applies to sacred texts independently of their oral or literary form of transmission. Sacred texts, therefore, are exempt from the pressure to adapt to the hermeneutical conditions of a changing world.

In the process of secondary canonization, the principle of sacred fixation is applied to *cultural* texts. On the one hand, they are treated like verbal temples enshrining divine presence, but on the other hand, they require understanding and application in order to exert their formative and normative impulses and demands. The solution of this problem is exegesis. Exegesis, or hermeneutics, is the successor of *mouvance*. In the *mouvance* stage of literate transmission, the commentary is being worked into the fabric of the text. This method has been shown by Michael Fishbane to be typical of the Biblical texts in their formative phase.[19] They are full of glosses, pieces of commentary which later redactors have added to the received text. Only with the closure of the canon is this process stopped, and thenceforth exegesis must take the form of a commentary that stays outside the text itself.[20]

This distinction between text and commentary, typical of secondary canonization, applies not only to the sacred but also to the classical canon. In this respect, the Alexandrian *philologoi* seem to have led the way. They introduced into their collection of ancient writings the distinction between *hoi prattómenoi* and all other texts, meaning by *prattómenoi* literally 'those to be treated,' the classical texts worthy of exegetical treatment—that is, a commentary.[21] The Latin author Aulus Gellius compared this textual elite to the highest class of Roman taxpayers, called *classici*. In the Jewish tradition, this split into text and commentary and the relationship between them, typical of secondary canonization, finds its earliest expression in the concept of a "written" and an "oral Torah" (*torah she be'al khitav* and *torah she be'al peh*). Here, commentary has to be oral in order not to violate the realm of writing, which is exclusively reserved for and occupied by sacred scripture. The oral Torah is a collection of oral debates and commentaries on the written Torah that itself became codified in the Talmudic and Midrashic traditions. It is believed to go back via an unbroken 'chain of reception' (*shalshelet ha-qabbalah*) to Moses himself.

The oral exegesis of a sacred text accompanying its public recitation seems indeed to correspond to Jewish custom dating back to the beginnings of canonization. Nehemiah reports a public reading of the Torah, where Ezra read the text and several of the Levites gave a commentary.

And Ezra opened the book in the sight of all the people, for he was above all the people, and as he opened it all the people stood. And Ezra blessed the LORD, the great God, and all the people answered, "Amen, Amen," lifting up their hands. And they bowed their heads and worshiped the LORD with their faces to the ground.

Also Jeshua, Bani, Sherebiah, Jamin, Akkub, Shabbethai, Hodiah, Maaseiah, Kelita, Azariah, Jozabad, Hanan, Pelaiah, the Levites, helped the people to understand the Law, while the people remained in their places. They read from the book, from the Law of God, clearly, and they gave the sense, so that the people understood the reading. (Neh. 8:5–8)

Some centuries later, the Jewish historian Flavius Josephus testifies to the same custom, where he compares Jewish and Greek religion.

Can any government be more holy than this? or any Religion better adapted to the nature of the Deity? Where, in any place but in this, are the whole People, by the special diligence of the Priests, to whom the care of public instruction is committed, accurately taught the principles of true piety? So that the body-politic seems, as it were, one great Assembly, constantly kept together, for the celebration of some sacred Mysteries. For those things which the Gentiles keep up for a few days only, that is, during those solemnities they call Mysteries and

Initiations, we, with vast delight, and a plenitude of knowledge, which admits of no error, fully enjoy, and perpetually contemplate through the whole course of our lives.[22]

It is obvious that Josephus, in this polemical passage, does not do full justice to the Greek organization of cultural memory. He ignores the classical canon, the traditions of scientific discourse, and the various forms of exegesis practiced in the schools of philosophy, medicine, and other branches of knowledge. He focuses only on religion, comparing the Jewish institutions of religious instruction and the Greek mystery cults. Arbitrary and highly selective as this comparison may be, it illustrates a very important distinction: the distinction between ritual and textual continuity.[23]

In spite of their extensive use of writing, Egyptian and other "pagan" religions were still relying on ritual continuity. In the world of ritual continuity, the public does in fact have to wait for the next performance in order to get access to the sacred texts of cultural memory. Textual continuity is only achieved when institutions of learning and exegesis are established that keep the ancient texts constantly present and semantically transparent. The transition from ritual to textual continuity means a complete reorganization of cultural memory, in the same way that the transition from the ethnically and culturally determined religions of the ancient world to the new type of transcultural and transnational world religions meant a totally new construction of identity. The canon, in a way, functioned as a new transethnic homeland and as a new transcultural instrument of formation and education.

There seems to exist a strong alliance between revelation, transcendence, and secondary canonization. The codification of revelation leads to an expatriation of the holy from worldly immanence into transcendence and into scripture. The pagan or pre-axial cult religions presuppose the immanence of the holy in images, trees, mountains, springs, rivers, heavenly bodies, animals, human beings, and stones. All this is denounced as idolatry by the new scripture-based world religions. Scripture requires a total reorientation of religious attention, which was formerly directed toward the forms of divine immanence and is now directed toward scripture and its exegesis. Secondary canonization means an exodus both of the holy and of religious attention from the cosmos into scripture. To the extra-mundane nature of God corresponds the textual character of his revelation.

"The Age of Transcendence," to use Benjamin Schwartz's beautiful term for the Axial Age,[24] saw the appearance of the "great individuals" who discovered in transcendental visions a world of absolute truth beyond this world of conditioned compromise. As far as the "great individuals" are concerned, the theory does not stand up to criticism. As has been shown above, Akhenaten, who has every claim to be included in this number, lived as early as the fourteenth century BCE. Moses, if he ever lived, must equally belong to that time, to which Zoroaster is now also dated by most scholars, whereas there is no reason why Jesus and Muhammad, who came much later, should be excluded. I do not want to belittle the groundbreaking achievements of these thinkers; in terms of their influence in shaping the world in which we are still living, the decisive event is not their terrestrial existence, but the canonization of their writings. The real "Axial Age" is not the age of the great individuals such as Zoroaster, Moses, Homer, Isaiah, Plato, Confucius, Buddha, and the like, who did not wait until 800 BCE to appear and who did not disappear by 200 BCE, but the age of secondary canonization. Canonization, as we have seen, is not an individual process, but a social and collective one. Canonization is the achievement of a society that decides to hold these texts in the greatest authority, to make them the basis of its life or to follow their model in artistic creation. There were presumably always great individuals with "transcendental visions." The decisive act is the step to turn these visions into "cultural texts," to select these texts into a canon, and to frame the transmission of this canon by institutions of exegesis ensuring its availability, readability, and authority over three thousand years. This was the achievement of the years from about 200 BCE to 200 CE when the great canons were established: the Confucian, the Taoist, and the Buddhist canons in the east, and the Avesta, the Hebrew Bible, and the canon of Greek "classics" in the west. All these breakthroughs are related to social, political, and spiritual crises, and all presuppose, of course, the necessary preconditions for establishing textual continuity. The Axial Age, in a way, is a "media event." Without the invention of writing, without the use of writing for the codification of cultural memory, and without the processes of canonization, the Axial Age would never have occurred. The Axial Age is nothing else but the formative phase of the textual continuity that is still prevailing in our western and eastern civilizations.

It was my intention to "deconstruct" to a certain degree the concept of the Axial Age, because it excludes figures such as Akhenaten and Muhammad with its fixation on the middle of the first millennium BCE, and because it precludes any hermeneutical approach to earlier civilizations with its ideas of a cultural mutation of man, a quantum leap in intellectual and spiritual orientation. I do not deny that a categorical transformation took place in the ancient world with its turn from cosmotheism to monotheism, from mythos to logos, from tribal society to complex forms of social and political organization, but I do not believe that all these changes took place more or less at the same time and were symptoms of a "mutation" of the human being into *homo sapiens axialis*, "the human being with whom we are still living." The concept of an Axial Age both overrates and underrates difference. It overrates the difference between archaic civilization and the modern mind, and it underrates the differences between the different "axial" civilizations as well as between the first millennium BCE and our modern age. Jaspers's concept of the Axial Age is not a theory but a scientific myth. By highlighting the importance of literacy and canonization, I wanted to de-dramatize and de-mythologize the concept. We are dealing here not with a mutation, but with an evolution stretching over several millennia, implying various historical factors and agents and implying even reversibility, backward movements of devolution or "de-axialization," as has been rightly stressed by Shmuel Eisenstadt on various occasions. The features of axiality, however, such as reflexivity, individuality, interiority ("inner man"), distancing from the world, progress in abstraction and intellectuality, "theory," critique of tradition, differentiation, "transcendental" concepts or visions—ideas and inventions with a tendency to global diffusion that have been brought up in the still ongoing discussion of Jaspers's theory—have proved indispensable tools of cultural analysis. They do not occur all at once, setting off a new world against the old, but occur here and there, in different forms, at different time periods, creating differences and similarities, and thereby enabling comparison and understanding.

6

EGYPTIAN MYSTERIES AND SECRET SOCIETIES IN THE AGE OF ENLIGHTENMENT

The "Mystery Fever" in the Late Eighteenth Century

The eighteenth century was not only the Age of Enlightenment but also the age of secret societies—two apparently opposed tendencies, for we would normally associate light with publicity and secrecy with darkness and occultism. A missing link, however, is provided by a contemporary, and at that time novel, theory about the ancient mysteries, especially the Egyptian mysteries, that was first expounded by William Warburton in about 1740, but did not gain wide acceptance or begin to exert a domineering influence until a generation later, after Warburton's work was translated into German by Johann Christian Schmidt. It enjoyed an enthusiastic reception by leading historians as well as prominent members and founders of secret societies after 1776.[1]

The English theologian, classicist, and Shakespeare scholar William Warburton published his monumental *Divine Legation of Moses* in several volumes between 1738 and 1741, the second book of which was dedicated to the ancient mysteries. The German philosopher and historian Christoph Meiners adopted Warburton's theory in his book *Über die Mysterien der Alten* ("On the Mysteries of the Ancients"), which, in its turn, was used as a blueprint by Adam Weishaupt for the establishment of his new order of the Illuminati.[2]

Between 1775 and 1800, there appeared several dozen scholarly dissertations on the ancient mysteries, as well as a similar number of novels, stories, plays, and operas dealing with the Egyptian and other mysteries, initiations, and secret communities. The most prominent representatives of this preoccupation are Mozart's and Schikaneder's *The Magic Flute*, Schiller's ballad "Das verschleierte Bild zu Sais" ("The Veiled Image at Sais"), and Goethe's *Wilhelm Meisters Lehrjahre*.[3]

In what respect can this novel theory about the ancient mysteries pass for a missing link between enlightenment and secrecy? And what, in the first place, is it all about; what is the novelty of it? The first question is easily answered: it is the obvious parallel between enlightenment and initiation. In the process of initiation, the candidate is enlightened about things he previously did not know. This analogy may explain the enormous boom of *Bildungsromane* (education novels) in the eighteenth century, starting with *Les aventures de Télémaque* by Fénelon (1699), many of which integrate into the educational career of their hero an initiation into a secret community. The second question requires a more detailed answer.

The innovative and enormously successful and influential element of the new theory about the ancient mysteries was the political interpretation it presented concerning their genesis and function. Warburton argued that the mysteries were co-emergent with the state. In its original form, before the emergence of the state, religion consisted in the worship of Nature as the sole deity. With the creation of the state, this original monotheism of Nature had to be turned into a mystery religion and practiced in secrecy, because the state had to be founded on a quite different religious system. Egypt, which was held to be the first state in the sense of a large-scale political organization in the history of mankind, presented the model for this double religion, which was followed by all the other nations: an official, public polytheism, and a mystery religion with secret rites and an arcane monotheistic or pantheistic theology, which then became the matrix of all other mystery cults.

Warburton's argument ran like this: The original religion of Nature was incapable of supporting the new political institution. A state and civil society cannot be based on natural theology; instead, it needs personal gods to protect the laws and to express national identity. People would not respect the laws if they had no fear of punishing and rewarding gods, nor would they have any sense of moral and political orientation without city gods and national gods. Any society aiming at social order and political power is therefore bound to invent a pantheon of tutelary deities, turning meritorious lawgivers, culture-founders, heroes, chiefs, and kings into gods and assigning them functions in the supervision of the laws and the symbolization of political and social identities. These deities are fiction, but a legitimate fiction, because they are indispensable in serving their purpose of providing justice and social order.

The original religion, however, the monotheism of Nature, could not be discarded, because it was known to be true and sanctified by tradition. Since it could not possibly coexist side by side with the newly established political religion of personal deities, because it would expose their purely fictional character, it had to be preserved, practiced, and transmitted clandestinely. The solution that the Egyptians found to that problem was twofold. They invented two scripts, one public, one secret, in order to separate everyday communication from the codification and transmission of the arcane rituals and theology. They also developed two forms of architecture, one above and one below ground, one for the monumental representation of the state and its public religion and one for the secret continuation of the natural religion, now become a mystery religion requiring long phases of initiation, instruction, and probation. The material evidence of this strange theory will be dealt with below as its "grammatological" and its "topological" basis.

Warburton built his theory on two ancient traditions. One is Varro's concept of the tripartite theology *(theologia tripertita)* with its distinction between natural, political, and poetical theology, which had already appeared in the seventeenth century in the form of a dichotomy of natural and political theology. The other is the Platonic distinction between the masses, on the one hand, who are unfit for abstract thinking and need fables and allegories to catch a glimpse of the truth, and the philosophers, on the other hand, who leave the cave of popular illusions and seek the light of true knowledge. The two traditions were already fused in the seventeenth century by scholars such as John Selden, Ralph Cudworth, and John Spencer into the concept of a split culture or *religio duplex*, with a popular, polytheistic, and exoteric outside and an arcane, monotheistic, or pantheistic and esoteric inside.[4] Alexander Ross, in his book *Pansebeia* (1652), a work of comparative religion,[5] even interpreted the pagan religions as political theology, opposing it, however, not to the natural theology of the mystery religions but to the truth of Biblical religion. "All false Religions," Ross wrote, "are grounded upon humane Policy to keep people in obedience and awe of their superiors."[6] It was Warburton's ground-breaking innovation to give the traditional concept of double religion and split culture a political interpretation and to concede a kind of truth even to the esoteric side of pagan religion. Moreover, he acquitted popular religion and political theology of any charge of conscious fraud (as most notoriously raised by Bernard de Fontenelle in his *Histoire des oracles*, 1687), arguing that although we are indeed dealing here with fictions, they are legitimate fictions because they are indispensable for any civil society and lawful political organization.

Before entering any further into the theory of Warburton and his followers on ancient mysteries, let it be absolutely clear that it is of no real historical interest whatsoever as far as ancient Egypt and antiquity in general is concerned. It cannot tell us anything about the historical mystery cults in antiquity, but very much about the intellectual situation of the eighteenth century with its political, social, and religious tensions, the cultural context in which the secret societies mushroomed and flourished and in which the topics of initiation and mystery played such an important role in literature and the arts. The theory of Warburton, Meiners, and all the others, which associated the state and the sphere of politics in general with the imaginary and with fictional institutions, and the sphere of mystery, esotericism, and concealment with truth and enlightenment, is rather absurd if applied to ancient history, but it is highly important and revealing when applied to the social and intellectual history of the eighteenth century. The image that the eighteenth century formed of ancient Egypt as a split civilization, divided into an exoteric and an esoteric culture, is interesting, not because it contained any authentic knowledge about Egypt but because it served as a mirror of contemporary society and culture.

The interest, even fascination, of the eighteenth century with ancient Egypt was focused on initiation. It was not only the idea of a split culture, but also and above all the path that led from the exoteric to the esoteric side, and the transformation that the initiate had to undergo in pursuing this path, that formed the central object of research. The ancient sources presented the Egyptian initiation in two aspects: grammatological and topological. The grammatological aspect pointed to the fact that in Egypt two different scripts were in use, one open, one secret. The topological aspect highlighted the number and size of subterranean constructions and held that the buildings above ground served the official popular religion, while the constructions underground, by contrast, served the secret religion. Both were based on severe misunderstandings of the Egyptian evidence.

The Imagined "Egyptian Mysteries" and Their Grammatological and Topological Basis

I shall only very briefly touch upon the well-known grammatological theories about hieroglyphs. Knowledge of hieroglyphs died out in Egypt during the fourth century CE, but a wealth of information concerning the Egyptian script persisted in Greek literature.[7] The Greeks were fascinated by hieroglyphic writing for two reasons: one is the iconic character of the signs and their apparent reference to things and concepts rather than to words and sounds, and the other is the fact that there existed, alongside hieroglyphic writing, another completely different and non-iconic script that was understood by the Greeks as being alphabetic. Both reasons were wrong but enormously influential for the image of Egypt in European memory.[8] Of the various authors highlighting the iconic, non-discursive, and purely conceptual character of the hieroglyphs, I quote here only a passage from Diodorus that insists on three points: the non-discursivity (the hieroglyphs do not render the order of speech), the metaphorical character of the meanings of depicted objects, and the emphasis on knowledge and memory. The mastery of the script requires a vast knowledge about the hidden meaning of things. Learning to read and write amounts to an initiation into the secrets of nature.

The distinction between the two scripts goes back to Herodotus, who visited Egypt in the middle of the fifth century BCE, and is most clearly expressed by Diodorus in the introduction to his passage on hieroglyphs mentioned above:

> The Egyptians use two different scripts: one, called "demotic," is learned by all; the other one is called "sacred." This one is understood among the Egyptians exclusively by the priests who learn them from their fathers in the mysteries.[9]

The existence of two different scripts is explained by the distinction between the sacred and the profane, priests and laymen, secrecy and publicity. Later sources, especially Clement of Alexandria and Porphyry, explicitly declare that the various steps in the acquisition of literacy, leading from the demotic to the sacred cursive and from there to the most accomplished script, the hieroglyphic cryptography, amounted to a veritable initiation. Pythagoras, for example, according to Porphyry, spent twenty years in Egypt entering into the various secrets of the different Egyptian scripts.[10] This grammatological interpretation of the Egyptian split culture forms the basis of the curious theory of dual religion or society. The use of two apparently different scripts reflected, in the eyes of the ancients, a split in Egyptian society, between the initiated priests, on the one hand, and the rest of literate society, on the other. This situation was a perfect confirmation of what Heliodorus and other ancient authors described as the Egyptian "duplex philosophy," a vulgar or exoteric and an exclusive or esoteric one, one for the people and one for the priests.

Hieroglyphic writing, therefore, was held to be not only a system of communication but also, and above all, a codification of sacred knowledge and divine wisdom. It was both natural and cryptic, whereas alphabetic writing was held to be both conventional and clear. The non-iconic, demotic script was believed to be an alphabet invented by the Egyptians for the purposes of communication, administration, and documentation, whereas hieroglyphs were invented for the purposes of mystery, for the transmission of esoteric knowledge. Needless to say, all this is pure imagination. Its importance lies not in what it has to say about ancient Egypt but about western concepts of secrecy, its religious and cultural functions.

The most important source in early modernity concerning the Egyptian hieroglyphs was the first book on hieroglyphs by Horapollo Nilotes, which dates from the fifth century and was discovered in 1418 by an Italian merchant in a Greek monastery.[11] For seventy hieroglyphs, it gives not only the meaning, which is mostly correct, but also the motivation, which is rather fantastic. The sign for 'to open' is said to be written with the image of a hare because this animal never closes its eyes, and the image of a goose portrays the word 'son,' because this bird has a special sense of family. Obviously, the lost knowledge about the phonetic meaning of the signs—the words for 'to open' and 'son' are nearly homonymous with the words for 'hare' and 'goose'—has been replaced with that moralizing zoology that is known to us from Aelian, Pliny, and the *Physiologus*.

Another discovery of the fifteenth century opened a window on the content of Egyptian esoteric knowledge believed to have been committed to hieroglyphs. This was the *Corpus Hermeticum*, which was brought to Florence after the fall of Constantinople and put on the desk of Marsilio Ficino: a collection of theo-philosophical treatises attributed to Hermes Trismegistus, a mythical Egyptian sage of remotest antiquity.[12] The quintessence of the Hermetic doctrine can be summarized in the motto *Hen kai pan*, 'One-and-All,' the equation of God with the world, a kind of mystical pantheism. Within this theological framework, cosmology becomes theology and scientific knowledge acquires theurgical or magical aspects since it operates on the divine powers immanent in nature. This is the practical branch of Hermeticism known as 'alchemy.' Giordano Bruno stressed the magical and mnemonic potentials of hieroglyphs as compared to alphabetic writing.

> The sacred letters used among the Egyptians were called hieroglyphs
> . . . which were images . . . taken from the things of nature, or their
> parts. By using such writings and voices, the Egyptians used to capture
> with marvellous skill the language of the gods. Afterwards when let-
> ters of the kind which we use now with another kind of industry were
> invented by Theuth or some other, this brought about a great rift both
> in memory and in the divine and magical sciences.[13]

Warburton will later follow Bruno in this reconstruction of the history of Egyptian written culture. Hieroglyphs came first; the aniconic writing was a later invention. However, Warburton corrected Bruno, Athanasius Kircher, and others in rightly stating that hieroglyphs were originally a quite normal script serving the normal purposes of written communication and data storage. Only later, when together with the state the mysteries were founded, was the hieroglyphic script turned into a cryptography, whereas the aniconic and seemingly alphabetic script was created for profane use.

Due to the connection between hieroglyphs and Hermeticism, the study of Egyptian hieroglyphs had, in addition to its grammatological, semiotic, and artistic implications, strong and far-reaching theological consequences. These became particularly obvious in the context of the debate about pantheism, atheism, and monotheism (all these terms were coined in this context) following the publication of Spinoza's *Ethica* and the rise of English Deism, which lent fresh color to the image of ancient Egypt and its mysteries. The arcane theology of Egypt was now interpreted as a kind of Spinozism *ante Spinozam*, and since Spinozism was anathema to official religion, the parallel between ancient Egypt and modern Europe became even closer.

The topological aspect of the Egyptian initiation to which we will turn now is much less prominently presented in the ancient (Greek and Latin) sources than the grammatological one, but plays a much greater role in the imagination of the eighteenth century. This is certainly due to the wealth of new information from travelers' reports and picture books about the archaeology of ancient Egypt. In its topological aspect, the Egyptian initiation assumes the form of a descent into the depths of the earth. The most prominent ancient travelers into the netherworld, Orpheus and Aeneas, play a certain role in the reconstruction of the Egyptian initiation: Orpheus because he is associated with the Orphic hymns, some of which proclaim the theology of the One-and-All, and Aeneas because his descent is explicitly associated with the Eleusinian initiation when Virgil has Hecate cry "Procul, o procul este, profani!" ('Keep off, keep off, ye profane!')—the traditional Eleusinian warning "Thyras d'epitheste bebeloi" ('Shut the doors [from outside], ye profane').[14] The most important source, however, is the encrypted report that, in the *Golden Ass* by Apuleius, Lucius gives of his initiation into the mysteries of Isis. Let us have a brief look at the famous lines.

> *Accessi confinium mortis*
> *et calcato Proserpinae limine*
> *per omnia vectus elementa remeavi*
> *nocte media vidi solem*
> *candido coruscantem lumine*
> *deos inferos et deos superos accessi coram*
> *et adoravi de proxumo.*

> I approached the border of death
> and set my foot on the threshold of Proserpina.
> After having traversed all of the elements I returned.
> In the middle of the night I saw the sun
> sparkling in white light.
> I approached the infernal and the supernal gods face to face
> and worshiped in close proximity.[15]

Three motifs will return in the eighteenth century: the association of initiation and death, travel through the four elements, and the vision of the gods.

The first modern author to transform these scant allusions into a detailed narrative of the Egyptian initiation was the Abbé Jean Terrasson, professor of Greek at the Collège de France and renowned editor of Diodorus of Sicily, who, in his novel *Séthos*, published in 1731, dedicated almost a hundred pages to the description of the initiation of his hero into the mysteries of Isis.[16] Sethos is the legitimate heir to the throne of Egypt who is, however, suppressed by his evil stepmother, Queen Daluca.

When he turns sixteen, his mentor Amedes concedes to his ardent wish to be initiated into the mysteries. Here we already see the contrast between corrupt public government and truthful secret religion. Sethos and Amedes enter the Great Pyramid on the north side and climb down into a very deep pit. Below, they traverse some passages and arrive at a portal with an inscription that will return verbatim in *The Magic Flute*.[17] Amedes is to stay behind and Sethos must pursue his path alone. He is received by three armed men, who warn him that there will be no return if he continues farther, and he is secretly guided and watched in a way that will be the role of the three boys in *The Magic Flute*. After several turns and passages he has to cross a room full of fire and swim through a channel of water. The last trial involves the air: he has to catch rings that will transport him with enormous noise through the air into the temple of Ptah and in front of the veiled image of Isis. The high priest greets him with a prayer that will also reappear in *The Magic Flute* almost verbatim. Sethos is given a drink that will cause him to forget all false ideas that he has formed during his former life and to remember all the instructions that he is going to receive during his subsequent initiation.

Terrasson presented his novel as the translation of an ancient Greek manuscript, which he even equipped with scholarly footnotes, and due to his high reputation as a scholar, his account of the Egyptian initiation was almost universally received as authentic. Several of its ideas became fixed stereotypes in the prolific literary production that followed in the wake of Terrasson's *Sethos*: ancient Egypt being completely undermined by subterranean constructions serving the functions of the arcane religion of Nature; the initiation as a transition from the upper world of illusions into the underworld of truth; and especially the Hermetic cave in which Hermes Trismegistus has stored the pillars inscribed with the primal, antediluvian wisdom of Adam. The most impressive description of the Hermetic cave is to be found in the *Athenian Letters*:

> The strange solemnity of the place must strike everyone, that enters it, with a religious horror; and is the most proper to work you up into that frame of mind, in which you will receive, with the most awful reverence and assent, whatever the priest, who attends you, is pleased to reveal. . . .
>
> Towards the farther end of the cave, or within the innermost recess of some prodigious caverns, that run beyond it, you hear, as it were

a great way off, a noise resembling the distant roarings of the sea, and sometimes like the fall of waters, dashing against rocks with great impetuosity. The noise is supposed to be so stunning and frightful, if you approach it, that few, they say, are inquisitive enough, into those mysterious sportings of nature. . . .

Surrounded with these pillars of lamps are each of those venerable columns, which I am now to speak of, inscribed with the hieroglyphical letters with the primeval mysteries of the Egyptian learning. . . . From these pillars, and the sacred books, they maintain, that all the philosophy and learning of the world has been derived.[18]

Ancient Egypt was now viewed not only as the origin of all ancient states and religions, including Biblical monotheism, but also as the mirror of modern society, with its exterior face of Church and absolutism and its interior of deism and enlightened philosophy. The Masons viewed themselves as the heirs of the Egyptian priests and of the ancient mystery religions, and the Egyptian mysteries were now studied as a model of modern Freemasonry. The most prolific center for this kind of research and literature was the lodge Zur Wahren Eintracht (True Concord) at Vienna, which made the systematic exploration of the ancient mysteries its central project and published during the years 1784 and 1787 no fewer than fourteen articles and longer dissertations in its *Journal für Freymäurer*.[19] One of the most interesting of these is an anonymous essay on the question of "scientific Freemasonry." The essay is generally attributed to Ignaz von Born, the master of the lodge, but the minutes confirm that a certain Anton Kreil presented two lectures on the same topic—the question of scientific Freemasonry—at the sessions of 16 and 22 April 1785, and it is beyond any doubt that he is the author of the published article.[20] Kreil was a highly educated philosopher and philologist who contributed several particularly interesting articles to the *Journal* and who created the term "scientific Freemasonry" as the opposite of "religious freemasonry," the first being the stronghold and promoter of enlightenment, the other of spiritual conservatism. The most interesting aspect of his lectures is the date of their delivery, for the minutes state that these were the sessions during which Leopold Mozart was elevated to the rank of Fellow and Master respectively, his son Wolfgang being present.[21] If anybody doubts that Mozart could have had any contact with the scholarly theories about the Egyptian mysteries, here is definite proof to the contrary. Kreil's lectures turn out to be the most impressive and colorful description of the Egyptian mysteries in their topological aspect, because he is among the first to take into account the archeological evidence. Comparing these reports with the theory of ancient Egypt's dual philosophy, he concludes that the extended subterranean structures with which the whole of Egypt is undermined—passages, corridors, pillared halls, sunken courtyards, rooms, and staircases—all of them inscribed with hieroglyphs from floor to ceiling, could serve but one purpose: to accommodate the libraries, laboratories, cult places, and ritual installations for the performance and transmission of the secret religion with its esoteric natural theology. The Egyptian priestly order, Kreil writes, was in possession of the collected wisdom of the ancients, and the Greeks, such as Pythagoras, Plato, and Eudoxus, went there to study the true philosophy. The priests spent most of their time underground studying the secrets of nature and theology and shrouded their knowledge in the impenetrable veils of hieroglyphs and hidden architecture. They were so successful in this that their tradition of wisdom persists in certain lodges until this day. It is on this occasion that Mozart may have first conceived the idea of bringing the Egyptian mysteries to the stage and translating the concept of dual religion into the form of a dual opera, with a popular exterior and a philosophical interior. When six years later he finally realized this project together with Emanuel Schikaneder, the result became the most prominent example of the new genre of mystery travels into the Egyptian underworld and the most convincing aesthetic representation of the Egyptian initiation.

Mozart entered the lodge named Zur Wohlthätigkeit (Beneficence) in 1784 and remained a dedicated Mason until his death, even in times when Freemasonry was no longer fashionable and membership in lodges became suspicious. That *The Magic Flute* is a Masonic opera is well known and becomes particularly obvious in the light of Warburton's political interpretation of mystery religion, which the Masons fully adopted. Warburton distinguished not only between the official, exoteric and the secret, esoteric religion, but within the esoteric religion between the Lesser and the Greater Mysteries. This distinction was practiced in the Eleusinian mysteries, which Warburton, following Diodorus, held to be merely a copy of the Egyptian mysteries. In a dual society, the way of initiation leads from the illusions of popular religion, through the darkness of disillusionment, probation, instruction, and trial, finally to the full light of the truth.

The Masonic theory reconstructs this passage *per aspera ad astra*, from darkness to light, in three stages: the purification or disillusionment, the Lesser Mysteries, and the Greater Mysteries. The Lesser Mysteries consist of probation and instruction. Here, everyone is admitted who shows a sincere interest and who is innocent of any serious crimes. By contrast, only the very few who have a vocation to leadership and who excel through virtue and wisdom are admitted to the Greater Mysteries. The Greater Mysteries confront the candidate with imminent death and send him into a state of utmost fear and horror. This is how Plutarch describes the Greater Mysteries in a passage much quoted in the Masonic literature.

Here on earth the soul is without knowledge except at the moment of death. Then it suffers an experience similar to those who celebrate the Greater Mysteries. For this reason both the word 'to die' (τελευταν) and the action which it denotes are the same as the word 'to be initiated' (τελεισθαι) and the action denoted. The first stage is wandering astray, tiresome walking in circles, some frightening paths in darkness that lead nowhere. Then, immediately before the end, one is seized by every kind of terror, all is horror, shudder, trembling, sweat and amazement. At the end, however, a wonderful divine light comes to meet you; pure regions and blossoming meadows are there to greet you with sounds and dances and solemn sacred words and holy views. And there, the initiate, perfect by now, set free and loose from all bondage, walks about, crowned with a wreath, celebrating the festival together with the other sacred and pure people, and he looks down on the uninitiated, unpurified crowd in this world in mud and fog beneath his feet.[22]

Initial state	First stage of initiation	Second stage	Third stage
The illusions of folk religion	Purification (disillusionment: emancipation from illusions)	Lesser Mysteries: trials, instructions	Greater Mysteries: 1. Near-death experience (the "Sublime") 2. "Epopteia" (Grand Vision— unveiling the veiled Isis)

The Magic Flute and the Egyptian Mysteries

If we apply this scheme to Mozart's opera, we get a perfect fit.

Act One		Act Two	
First part	Second part	Third part	Fourth part
Overture and nos. 1–7 (duet)	Finale	No. 9 (march) through no. 20 (aria)	Finale
"Illusion/ mystification"	Disillusionment	Lesser Mysteries	Greater Mysteries
Tamino enters the realm of the Queen of the Night and adopts her views ("princess rescue story")	Tamino suspects the truth and turns into a "seeker"	(with Papageno) First trial (withstand 3 women) Second trial: keep silence toward the beloved (withstand the commands of love)	(without Papageno) Near-death experience (Pamina's attempted suicide, passage through fire and water, illumination)
E-flat major	C major	F major	E-flat major

The division into Lesser and Greater Mysteries corresponds to the first and the second part of the second act. The opera is divided into two acts, each of which is further divided into a first part, with arias and dialogue, and a second part, with a long continuous finale without any dialogue. Each part is of approximately equal length and ends in the key in which it started, which is E^b major for the first, C major for the second, F major for the third, and E^b major again for the fourth. The third part, which is the first part of the second act, contains the tests and instructions characteristic of the Lesser Mysteries; here, even Papageno is present, though his behavior during the trial is a rather poor performance. The theme here is self-control: the initiates must learn to resist their urge to communicate, and while Papageno fails to abstain from talking to Papagena, Tamino keeps silent before his beloved Pamina even in the face of her professions of pain and despair. The fourth part contains the Greater Mysteries; here, Papageno is absent, but Pamina joins Tamino before the trial of water and fire and attains the light of truth when the theater, as Schikaneder has it in his stage direction, "changes into a sun." The word 'death' is indeed the key word in this part, which begins with Pamina's attempted suicide, then shows Tamino before the "gates of dread, which threaten me with danger and death." "If he is able to overcome the horrors of death," the inscription above the portal reads, "he will ascend from earth to heaven." "By the power of music," they sing, "we happily walk through death's dark night." The point of the Greater Mysteries is to transform the personality of the initiate by exposing him to the fear of death, which is to say, to an experience of the sublime.

Once the two parts of the second act have been identified with the Lesser and Greater Mysteries, it is easy to recognize the stages of illusion and disillusionment in the first act. Tamino (and with him the audience) is first lured into the Queen of the Night's story of the abducted princess and must then, in the second part, undergo a thorough reorientation, which frees him from false presumptions but leaves him in the dark as to the truth. It is obvious that the opera attempts to present the Egyptian mysteries in their various contrasts and oppositions: folk religion and esoteric wisdom, superstition and truth, the world of illusions above and the subterranean realm of true knowledge.

Judging from the early stage designs, the action of *The Magic Flute* does not take place in ancient Egypt at all, but in some exotic region or Masonic park where the mysteries of Isis are still performed. Not ancient Egypt itself, but the Egyptian mysteries, which were held to be still alive among the Masons, formed the theme of the opera. It was only after the Napoleonic expedition to Egypt and the appearance of the lavish volumes of the *Description de l'Égypte* that the opera was staged in ancient Egyptian scenery.

Another member of the True Concord lodge, who took a leading part in the lodge's research project on the ancient mysteries, left Vienna just before Mozart joined the lodge, went to Leipzig and Weimar, then was offered a chair of philosophy at Jena and was influential in getting Schiller, whom he admired, appointed to a chair of history there. This was the young philosopher Carl Leonhard Reinhold, a leading figure of both Illuminism and German idealism. Reinhold, asked to contribute a study on the Hebrew mysteries for the Viennese project, read Warburton and especially Spencer and delivered an astonishing update of Spencer's thesis about the Egyptian origin of Mosaic monotheism.[23] Schiller was so fascinated by Reinhold's findings that he published an essay on the same subject: "Die Sendung Moses" (The Legation of Moses), which is just a summary of Reinhold's book.[24]

The thesis is that Moses learned everything about true religion in the Egyptian mysteries and that the religion he gave the Hebrews is but a popularized version of Egyptian esoteric Deism. The Egyptian deity is the All-One, the veiled goddess of the image at Sais, whose inscription reads, "I am all that was, is, and will be. No mortal has lifted my veil." This sublime deity, as Schiller stresses, has no name, because he/she is unique, is one-and-all, so that he/she should be named by every name or no name. Moses translates this idea into his concept of "Jehova" (Yahweh), which is equally not a name but the withholding of a name, meaning "I am that I am." Reinhold and Schiller follow the Septuagint's version in reading this as "I am the essential Being," which in their eyes says the same as "I am all that is."

However, since a state and civil society cannot be founded upon natural theology, Moses had to accommodate this sublime idea to the capacities of his people, and turn the god of the philosophers into a national god and into the fabulous "god of the fathers"—in other words, turn natural theology into political and mythical theology, according to Varro's concept of *theologia tripertita*.

Beethoven was so impressed by Schiller's essay that he copied some key sentences, such as "I am all that is," on a sheet of paper and put it in a frame on his desk.[25] Deism was the religion of enlightenment and it was believed to date back to the arcane theology of the Egyptian mysteries.

The secret, in its Masonic construction, was twofold. On the one hand, it was a secret, shut away from general knowledge because revealing it would have destroyed the fictions that supported the state and civil institutions. This was the political interpretation, which Warburton had promoted and which goes back to ancient and early modern religious critique. In this interpretation, the secret is principally knowable and actually known by the elite among the initiated. The secret is essentially negative: it consists in the fictional and illusionary character of religion. On the other hand, the secret enshrouds an unfathomable mystery. Its secrecy is not the result of political and social exclusivism, but of natural transcendence, in that it transcends human capacities of cognition, understanding, articulation, and communication. This is the positive aspect of the secret. There is something behind the veil which is more than fiction and illusion, but is beyond human understanding and even more than normal human beings can stand.

As the great French historian of philosophy Pierre Hadot has shown in his marvelous book *Le voile d'Isis*, the concept of the veiled image at Sais played a large role in eighteenth-century thought.[26] The mystery behind the veil was identified with the Egyptian goddess Isis and she, in turn, was interpreted as "Nature," not in its physical and phenomenal aspect as *natura naturata* but in its invisible, supernatural aspect as *natura naturans*, a mysterious transcendent power behind the phenomena which in turn were associated with the veil that simultaneously hides and manifests the deity. In frontispieces to works of natural science, the act of removing the veil of nature was a favorite allegory for scientific discovery. Even Heinrich Füssli reverted in 1808 to the iconography of unveiling Isis when he designed the frontispiece to *The Temple of Nature* by Erasmus Darwin, the grandfather of Charles Darwin.

The tradition goes back to Plutarch and his treatise *On Isis and Osiris*, in which he mentions the strange inscription in order to prove the enigmatic, mysterious character of Egyptian religion. "At Sais," he writes, "the seated statue *(tò hédos)* of Athena, whom they consider to be Isis, also bore the following inscription: 'I am all that has been and is and shall be; and no mortal has ever lifted my garment *(tòn emòn péplon)*.'"[27] Since Marsilio Ficino, Plutarch's 'peplos' has generally been translated as 'veil.' The initiated priests in Egypt who pursued their worship underground performed the mysteries of Isis or Nature. This was the true religion, which had to be kept secret, and Isis-Nature was the goddess behind the veil. This idea appealed to the Freemasons, most of whom were alchemists or mineralogists like Goethe or Ignaz von Born, the master of True Concord. In his dissertation on the Egyptian mysteries, von Born lets a priest summarize the ultimate aim of the Egyptian mysteries in the following words:

> The knowledge of nature is the ultimate purpose of our application. We worship this progenitor, nourisher and preserver of all creation in the image of Isis. Only he who knows the whole extent of her power and force will be able to uncover her veil without punishment.[28]

The first person plural in this quote could equally well apply to the Masons themselves.

Schiller treated this topos in his ballad "Das verschleierte Bild zu Sais." Driven by an insatiable thirst for knowledge, a youth, presumably Greek, travels to Sais in Egypt in order to be initiated into the mysteries and to look behind the veil that hides the image of truth or Isis in the innermost sanctuary of the temple. He is guided by a priest who has himself never enjoyed this view nor felt tempted to seek it. *Epopteia*, the view of truth, is something reserved for the very, very few. The youth, however, cannot master his curiosity. The next night, he enters the temple and removes the veil. In the morning, he is found prostrate on the floor. He is never able to tell of his experience, loses his good spirits, and dies soon afterward. It is clear that he saw something, but Schiller does not tell us what. From his other writings of that period, one may assume that he was exposed to a confrontation with the sublime. The sublime was defined as the absolutely overpowering experience that defies man's physical and intellectual capacities. Kant, in his third critique, distinguished these two expressions of the sublime as the "dynamic" and the "mathematical" sublime. Schiller proposed the distinction between the "theoretical sublime," transcending human imagination, and the "practical sublime," threatening with death the human drive for self-preservation. Both Kant and Schiller saw in the veiled image at Sais and its inscription the quintessential expression of the sublime. "There is," wrote Kant in his third critique, "no thought more sublime or more sublimely expressed than the famous inscription on the veiled image of Isis, i.e., Mother Nature, in her temple at Sais: I am all that was, is, and will be. No mortal has lifted my veil."[29]

In one of its latest applications, the motif of unveiling Isis was used as an allegory not of natural science but of the Napoleonic expedition to Egypt. This expedition was not only a military but also and above all a scholarly raid on ancient Egypt. Napoleon's army was accompanied by a legion of scholars, artists, and engineers with the mission of recording everything concerning modern and especially ancient Egypt. A special medal was issued in 1826 in commemoration of the publication of the *Description de l'Égypte*, which laid the foundations of modern Egyptology. On this medal, Egypt is personified by the recumbent woman whom the French soldier in Roman attire is unveiling. The inscription reads GALLIA VICTRICE AEGYPTUS REDIVIVA 1798 1826, "Egypt revivified through victorious France 1798. 1826." In 1822, exactly four hundred years after the arrival of Horapollo's *Hieroglyphica* in Florence, Jean-François Champollion succeeded in deciphering the hieroglyphs. With this achievement, ancient Egypt lost its mysteries. There is no monotheism, no arcane theology, no antagonism between a popular religion and a religion of the sages and initiates. The hieroglyphs were shown not to be a cryptography but the normal writing used for stone inscriptions, basically the same system as the cursive writings, and the subterranean structures were identified as tombs. Egyptology did in fact unveil and demystify ancient Egypt. A painting by François Picot dating from 1827 decorates the ceiling of a hall in the Louvre meant to host the collection of Egyptian antiquities that Champollion brought home from Egypt. It shows the unveiling of ancient Egypt before the eyes of Minerva, accompanied by the personifications of Art and Science.[30] Ancient Egypt lost her mystery after this definitive unveiling; it lives on only in the imagination of occultism. The rise of the bourgeoisie and the historical sciences marked the end of the alliance of secrecy and enlightenment, as well as of the ideal of a double philosophy.

7

TOTAL RELIGION: POLITICS, MONOTHEISM, AND VIOLENCE

The Concept of *Ernstfall*

The world is full of violence committed in the name of religion. Where does this violence come from? What does it have to do with religion? This is the question to which this last chapter will be dedicated. I speak from an Egyptologist's or antiquarian's point of view; I am asking about origins, not about contemporary movements, let alone about the future of religion. I will be going back in time, seeking the earliest occurrences of genuinely religious violence and their historical circumstances.

One source of religious violence, perhaps the decisive one, seems to me to consist in the polarizing power of religion, dividing people into Jews and gentiles, Christians and non-Christians, believers and non-believers, Muslims and Hindus, Catholics and Protestants, Sunni and Shi'i, orthodox and heretics, and it seems that the closer these groups are to each other, the greater the violence that might arise between them. As the driving force behind these divisions and subdivisions, I identified (in my book *Moses the Egyptian*) a new concept of absolute religious truth, based on a new distinction between truth and untruth which I called "The Mosaic Distinction," because I held that it was only monotheism that introduced this distinction into the realm of religion.[1] This thesis met with much objection, and with good reason: why should truth have anything to do with violence? An additional element is needed to explain the transformation of truth into violence, the transformation of the distinction between true and false religion into that of friend and foe.

As to the distinction between friend and foe, Carl Schmitt is the authority to turn to. Schmitt was a professor of constitutional law at Bonn and Berlin during the Weimar Republic, and later became the court lawyer, as it were, of the Third Reich. As such, he is a highly problematic figure and his theories must be handled very cautiously. The distinction between friend and foe is expounded by Schmitt in a book titled *Der Begriff des Politischen* (The Concept of the Political) that first appeared in 1928, five years before the Nazis came to power. I refer here to the second edition, published in 1932 and constantly reprinted since.[2] I do not agree with Schmitt's notion that the distinction of friend and foe is the principle of the political in general. For a theory of political violence, however, I think Schmitt has opened up a very promising approach. Let us, therefore, have a closer look at his argumentation.

Schmitt defines the political as the polarizing principle, dividing people into friend and foe. His thesis is that humans group themselves automatically according to this distinction. In normal life, however, this principle remains hidden. The 'other' appears as different and not-belonging, but not as 'foe.' We negotiate with the others, form contracts, cooperate, and communicate in the most varied ways. It is only the case of emergency *(Ernstfall)*, the case of war, that lays bare the true character of the principle of association and dissociation. In this argumentation, the concept of *Ernstfall*, or 'case of emergency,' is decisive. In what follows, I shall use the German word *Ernstfall*, because of its association with *ernst* (earnest), literally: the case of seriousness, when things turn serious, a notion that is much closer to what Schmitt has in mind than the term 'emergency,' for which the normal German word is *Notfall*. The concept of *Ernstfall* belongs to the radical style of thought that was typical of this time of expressionism and existentialism, especially in Germany. In the same way as Heidegger defined life as "being toward death" *(Sein zum Tode)*, Schmitt defines the political or the state as "being toward war." The truth of existence does not reveal itself in normal life but in the case of emergency, the *Grenzsituation* ('boundary situation'), as Jaspers put it. We are dealing here with a logic of escalation that defines the essence or nature of something with regard to its extreme state of intensity. The existentialist style of thought seems strange to us today, but for our question concerning the roots of violence, the logic of escalation and the concept of *Ernstfall* seem very useful. Before the outbreak of violence comes a process of escalation, when an existing distinction turns into polarization and polarization into open hatred and enmity. Convince people that the *Ernstfall* is imminent and they will be ready for every sacrifice, forget all other important bonds and differences, and know only friend and foe, against whom they are resolved to fight with all their might.

Schmitt proceeds in two steps. As a first step, he wants to isolate the political as an autonomous cultural sphere by means of defining a specific difference vis-à-vis other cultural spheres. Such spheres are based on distinctions such as good and evil (constituting the moral sphere), just and unjust (the sphere of law), gain and cost (the sphere of economy), truth and error (the sphere of science), art and non-art (the sphere of art), belief and unbelief (the sphere of religion), and friend and foe (the sphere of politics).[3] Such distinctions facilitate observation; they permit us to identify what can pass for political, moral, or aesthetic action, for example; they produce meaning and provide a rationale for an action that would otherwise be incomprehensible. Max Weber, Niklas Luhmann, and other theorists of modernity saw in these processes of differentiation the hallmark of modernity. These cultural spheres relativize each other: this is the new polytheism that Max Weber saw coming. For this reason, Schmitt defines modernity as "the age of neutralisations and de-politicisations."[4]

Yet Schmitt does not halt here. He wants not only to define, but to overcome modernity. For him, therefore, it is not sufficient to identify "the political" as an autonomous cultural domain, standing with equal right alongside the other domains. Rather, he wants to subordinate the other domains to the political.

With his distinction between friend and foe, he argues not for the *autonomy* but for the *hegemony* of the political. "The political," he writes,

> can draw its force from the most various domains of human life, from religious, economical, moral and other oppositions; it does not denote a domain of its own but rather the degree of intensity that an association or dissociation of humans may take on, whose motives may be of a religious, national, economical or other nature. . . . The real opposition of friend and foe is so strong and decisive that non-political, purely religious, purely cultural differences and motives fade into the background. In any event, political is an association under the sign of the *Ernstfall*. This, therefore, is the relevant, decisive form of human association.[5]

The "real possibility of the association according to friend and foe," Schmitt adds, "suffices to create beyond the purely social a normative form of unity that is something specifically different and decisive vis-à-vis the other associations. In reality, there is no political 'society' or 'association,' there is only one political unity, one political community."[6] This is Schmitt's definition of the difference between *Gesellschaft* and *Gemeinschaft*, society and community. Community is society under the conditions of the *Ernstfall*. The political, for this reason, is the totalizing principle overruling all other associations and spheres, on whatever distinctions they are based. In this treatise, Schmitt pleads for the total state that corresponds to the totalizing hegemony of the political.

It is the *Ernstfall* that grants the political this priority. Under the conditions of the *Ernstfall*, association becomes friendship, dissociation becomes enmity, society becomes community. *Ernstfall* means war; the war is the hour of truth, where the reality of existence, which is hidden in normal life, becomes revealed. The war reveals—'to reveal,' in Greek, is *apokalyptein*—the true nature of human community, which therefore must be defined with regard to war. With these arguments, Schmitt is fighting against modern liberalism and the differentiation of modern civilization into autonomous spheres such as art and science, law and economy, politics and religion. He wants the whole human being, the united people, the total state. Under normal, everyday conditions, the liberal differentiation of autonomous cultural spheres may be in order, but normality is an illusion that conceals the true nature and order of things. Only when things turn serious, in the *Ernstfall*, do reality and truth show their true face, and reality and truth must be the yardstick of conceptual clarity.

The Religious *Ernstfall*

Thus Carl Schmitt analyzes the political and its polarizing power. We know what terrible outbreaks of murderous violence this concept of the total state has led to. Let us now ask what we may learn from this analysis of religion and the kind of violence that emerges from its specific polarizing power. It is obvious that religions may also unite and separate, associate and dissociate people. Moreover, it is obvious that these unions and separations may assume different and at times dangerous degrees of intensity. It follows that there should also exist here a kind of *Ernstfall* in the light of which the criterion of association and dissociation takes on the character of friend and foe and leads to the outbreak of violence.

The first candidate for a specifically religious *Ernstfall* that comes to mind is the idea of the wrath of God, which either has already discharged itself in a terrible catastrophe or is imminent after some terrible religious crime. The history of religion is full of examples of divine wrath and punishment. Especially rich in this respect is the Hebrew Bible, beginning with the story of the Golden Calf and continuing with endless massacres and punishments up to the fall of Jerusalem.[7] All these Biblical examples fulfill two criteria that place them in the political sphere. First, they all belong within the frame of the idea of the covenant, the political alliance that God and the people have formed, where religious crime takes on the political character of defection, the breaking of a treaty. Second, all of them imply the employment of *human* violence that fights for God by identifying and eliminating defectors as enemies of God. This latter trait distinguishes this kind of violence from, for example, the ten Egyptian plagues by which God forces Pharaoh to let his people go. This is purely divine violence; humans do not intervene and there is no mention of divine wrath, no more than on the occasions of those other punishing actions of God that preceded the covenant: the expulsion of Adam and Eve from paradise, the banishment of Cain, the flood, the confusion of languages, the destruction of Sodom and Gomorrah. Human violence, however, is exactly what we are interested in, and this appears only after entering the covenant at Mount Sinai.

According to the unanimous opinion of Biblical scholars, the foundational text of Biblical covenant theology is the book of Deuteronomy. It is here, and in the most prominent place within this absolute centerpiece of Israelite religion, that we meet with the distinction between friend and foe.

I am Yahweh, thy God, who brought thee out of the land of Mizrayim, from the house of bondage.

Thou shalt have no other gods beside me.

Thou shalt not make for thyself any carved idol, or any likeness of anything that is in heaven above, or that is in the earth beneath, or that is in the water under the earth. You shall not bow down to them nor serve them, for I the LORD thy God am a jealous God, punishing the iniquity of the fathers upon the children to the third and the fourth generation of those who hate me, but showing mercy to the thousandth generation of those who love me and keep my commandments. (Deut. 5:6–10)

And again in the closing formula of the decalogue:

> Know therefore that the LORD, thy God, he is God, the faithful God, who keeps covenant and troth with those who love him and keep his commandments; and repays them that hate him to their face, to destroy them. (Deut. 7:9–10)

The wrath of God springs from his jealousy, which in its turn is associated with the ideas of covenant and loyalty that both partners of the covenant swore to each other. This jealousy, *qin'ah* in Hebrew, is a political affect that also motivates human action. God's jealousy and human zeal are expressed in Hebrew by the same word, *qin'ah*, in Greek *zēlos*. *Qin'ah* drives both the jealous God, El-Qanna', and the *qana'im*, zealots, who appropriate God's jealousy. This mirroring relationship between divine jealousy and human zeal finds its particularly clear expression in the story of Phinehas, the model of zealotry. Near the end of their forty years of wandering through the wilderness, the Israelites build their camp at Shittim, socialize with the men and especially the women of Moab, and take part in a feast in honor of Ba'al Pe'or, the local god. Furious about this act of infidelity, God sends a plague that kills twenty-four thousand people and only desists from his rage when Phinehas spears his compatriot Zimri and a Midianite woman in the act of making love.

> And the LORD spoke to Moses, saying: Phinehas, the son of Eleazar, the son of Aaron the priest has turned my wrath away from the children of Israel, in that he was zealous for my sake among them, that I consumed not the children of Israel in my jealousy. (Num. 25:11)

I am focusing here not on the plague and its twenty-four thousand victims; this is normal, so to speak, in the ancient world. I am focusing on the deed of Phinehas, who intervenes spontaneously for God: this is new, even revolutionary, and would have been impossible, I assert, in any other ancient culture.

The ideas of covenant and loyalty, in which the concepts of divine jealousy and human zeal are rooted, belong to the political sphere. From this source, therefore, originates the corresponding form of religious violence, zealotry. This has been demonstrated by recent research on Near Eastern sources. To a large degree, the Biblical concepts of covenant and loyalty are adopted from Neo-Assyrian royal ideology. Hittite and Assyrian vassal treaties and loyalty oaths served as models for the structure and content of Deuteronomy and Deuteronomy-inspired texts dealing with covenant and covenant ideology.[8] Some passages seem to be almost verbatim translations of Esarhaddon's loyalty oaths. Even the Hebrew term *b'rît*, 'covenant,' seems to translate Assyrian *adê* as a term not only for the alliance that Esarhaddon forms with his subjects and vassals, but for the one that the god Assur forms with Esarhaddon. In these oaths, absolute and exclusive loyalty is required, with all of one's heart, soul, and strength, and apostasy is sanctioned by the severest punishment.

We are dealing with the transposition of an originally political concept to the religious level, transforming god–king, king–subject, and king–vassal relations into the relations between god and man as well as God and Israel. This, however, means less a *translation* than an *inversion* of the original model. The conqueror who forces a conquered people into vassaldom turns into a liberator who offers the liberated people a treaty that it is free to accept or reject. Loyalty becomes fidelity, vassaldom becomes covenant, and politics becomes religion.

This is the temporal, political, ideological, and social context in which the idea of the covenant, together with its semantics of unconditioned fidelity and loyalty, arose. The temporal frame is defined by Israel's dependency on Assyria, the Northern Kingdom at the end of the eighth century BCE and the Southern Kingdom in the seventh century until its fall in 587 to the Babylonians, who succeeded the Assyrians.[9] Otherwise the textual borrowings of the Deuteronomic texts from Assyrian models cannot be explained. We are thus referred to a period of extreme suffering and pressure, full of violence, distress, and political tension. In Deuteronomy and Deuteronomistic history we perceive the voice of an opposition loyal to Yahweh, protesting against the royal policy of compromise and religious syncretism.

The Maccabean Wars: An Early Case of Religious Violence

Up to this point, we have been moving more in the realm of literature and ideas than in the realm of history that forms the context of this realm but not its content. There is no evidence whatsoever that these scenes of violence exerted in the name of God have any relation to historical events. The situation seems different, however, when in the year 165 BCE an incident occurs that explicitly repeats the exploit of Phinehas. Mattathias, the high priest, was ordered by an officer, a representative of the Seleucid government, to perform a pagan sacrifice; he refused, risking his life, but saw that another Jew hurried forward to carry out the required rite.

> And when Mattathias saw it, his zeal was kindled, and his heart quivered [with wrath]; and his indignation burst forth for judgment, so that he ran and slew him on the altar; and at the same time he [also] killed the king's officer who had come to enforce the sacrificing, pulled down the altar, and [thus] showed forth his zeal for the Law, just as Phinehas had done in the case of Zimri the son of Salu. And Mattathias cried out with a loud voice in the city, saying, "Let everyone that is zealous for the Law and that would maintain the covenant come forth after me!" And he and his sons fled unto the mountains, and left all that they possessed in the city. (1 Maccabees 2:24–28)

This is the beginning of the Maccabean revolt and the origin of zealotry, not as a literary motif but as a historical movement.

It appears, according to the books of Maccabees and in Flavius Josephus, that in Jerusalem during the first decades of the second century BCE the elite became inclined toward reform and toward opening the Jewish religion to international, Hellenistically stamped culture.[10] In pursuing these goals, they cooperated with the Seleucid government and pushed the king to issue a decree prohibiting the observance of the Jewish laws on penalty of death.

> that they should cease the . . . sacrifices, and drink offerings in the sanctuary, and that they should profane the Sabbaths and feasts, . . . and that they should sacrifice swine and [other] unclean animals; and that they should leave their sons uncircumcised, and make themselves abominable by means of [practicing] everything that was unclean and profane, so that they might forget the Law, and change all the [traditional] ordinances. And whosoever should not act according to the word of the king, should die. (1 Macc. 1:41–50)[11]

This is the historical situation constituting the *Ernstfall* that grouped the Jewish people into friend and foe and led to a civil war. For Judas Maccabeus fought not only a war of resistance against the Seleucid occupation, but also a civil war against his own people, extinguishing—if we may believe 1 Maccabees—the life of whole Jewish towns that adopted the "common way of life" (*ho koinós bíos*, after Josephus). In the same way as his father Mattathias followed the example of Phinehas, Judas Maccabeus based his strategy on Deuteronomy, chapters 13 and 20.

In Deuteronomy 20, a distinction is drawn between normal and exterminatory warfare. Normal rules of war apply to distant cities, which must be offered peace and submission before starting a siege; in the case of conquest, the male population may be killed, the women and children enslaved, and booty taken.

> When you draw near to a town to fight against it, offer it terms of peace. If it accepts your terms of peace and surrenders to you, then all the people in it shall serve you at forced labor. If it does not submit to you peacefully, but makes war against you, then you shall besiege it; and when the LORD your God gives it into your hand, you shall put all its males to the sword. You may, however, take as your booty the women, the children, livestock, and everything else in the town, all its spoil. You may enjoy the spoil of your enemies, which the LORD your God has given you. Thus you shall treat all the towns that are very far from you, which are not towns of the nations here. (Deut. 20:10–15)

In contrast, Canaanite cities that are nearby are not to be offered submission, but must be conquered and destroyed.

> But as for the towns of these peoples that the LORD your God is giving you as an inheritance, you must not let anything that breathes remain alive. You shall annihilate them—the Hittites and the Amorites, the Canaanites and the Perizzites, the Hivites and the Jebusites—just as the LORD your God has commanded, so that they may not teach you to do all the abhorrent things that they do for their gods, and you thus sin against the LORD your God. (Deut. 20:16–18)

This means that no living thing is to be left alive and no booty is to be taken, but everything must be burned in order to avoid contamination with Canaanite paganism. Chapter 13 prescribes the same treatment for Hebrew cities that have abandoned the law and taken up Canaanite mores.

> If you hear it said about one of the towns that the LORD your God is giving you to live in, that scoundrels from among you have gone out

and led the inhabitants of the town astray, saying, "Let us go and worship other gods," whom you have not known, then you shall inquire and make a thorough investigation. If the charge is established that such an abhorrent thing has been done among you, you shall put the inhabitants of that town to the sword, utterly destroying it and everything in it—even putting its livestock to the sword. All of its spoil you shall gather into its public square; then burn the town and all its spoil with fire, as a whole burnt offering to the LORD your God. It shall remain a perpetual ruin, never to be rebuilt. Do not let anything devoted to destruction stick to your hand, so that the LORD may turn from his fierce anger and show you compassion, and in his compassion multiply you, as he swore to your ancestors, if you obey the voice of the LORD your God by keeping all his commandments that I am commanding you today, doing what is right in the sight of the LORD your God. (Deut. 13:13–19)[12]

Judas and his followers already see in the emerging Hebrew Bible, the "scripture," the highly normative codification of the will of God that must be executed with fervent zeal.

To be zealous, however, does not only mean being ready to kill; it also means being ready to die. In the context of zealotry, murder and martyrdom are two sides of the same coin. Martyrdom (in Hebrew *qiddush ha-shem*, 'sanctifying the Name') is an innovation in the history of religion—not on the literary level, where one could perhaps refer to the tradition of the "servant of God" in Isaiah 53, but certainly on the level of history.[13] This has to be seen in close correlation with another innovation that coincides precisely with the Maccabean movement, a new concept of *Ernstfall* and revelation: the concept of paradise and the implied distinction between salvation and damnation. This distinction belongs within the frame of another semantics quite different from that of covenant theology, and the correspondent idea of *Ernstfall* is not the spontaneous wrath of God, a reaction to transgressions against the alliance, but the idea of a last judgment, the judgment of the world at the end of time, when God draws the final distinction between friend and foe, assigning the friends to paradise and the foes to hell.

It seems to me anything but a mere coincidence that the year 165 BCE saw not only the outbreak of the Maccabean revolt but also the emergence of Jewish apocalypticism. In this year, the Book of Daniel was written, the earliest apocalyptic text in Jewish tradition. For the apocalyptic semantics, the decisive scene, besides the two dreams revealing the course of history until the end of time, seems to me to be the writing on the wall with the image of the balance, on which Belshazzar is found to be too light and is discarded. This is the balance on which the world will be weighed and judged. Revelation means the disclosure of the *Ernstfall*, and this consists in the end and the judgment of the world as it is described or revealed in Matthew 25 and the Revelation of John. The decisive point is that the *Ernstfall* is revealed as immediately imminent.

He who knows for whom the bell tolls sees himself confronted with the decision to join the side of salvation or that of damnation. Now, in the light of this confrontation, the principle of religious association and dissociation reaches its "highest degree of intensity," in the words of Carl Schmitt. In the framework of the new semantics of apocalypticism, martyrdom provides the chance to opt, in a single step, to side with salvation and to immediately enter paradise.[14] If we understand revelation in this precise sense of apocalypse, revelation appears to be a totalizing principle, deriving its totalizing power from the real possibility of the Last Judgment. The concept of 'total religion' means a religion that claims hegemonic control of the whole of culture and the individual human being in the same way as Carl Schmitt defined the concept of the 'total state'; it bases its claim on its specific religious idea of *Ernstfall*, the apocalypse or revelation. This concept establishes religion as both an autonomous and a hegemonic sphere, dominating and controlling all other cultural spheres.

We now see more clearly, I think, what could be defined as *Ernstfall* in the realm of religion, and we can now distinguish two concepts of *Ernstfall*. One is the covenant concept according to which the *Ernstfall* is imminent when a religious crime, a break of covenant in the eyes of God, occurs; this type of *Ernstfall* consists in the wrath of God. The other and much more radical type is the concept of apocalypse, where the *Ernstfall* is defined as the end of the world and the Last Judgment. In the same way as politics in Schmitt's definition, religion, too, appears as a matter of identity and belonging, of association and dissociation, the single but decisive difference being that God is included as a partner.

Under the condition of *Ernstfall*, religion—in the same way as politics—raises a totalizing claim, requiring hegemony over all the domains of culture. This applies even to politics; the political form of total religion is theocracy.

This form of religion is based on another radical innovation in history, the idea of 'God's own or chosen people.' Belonging to or being loyal to God is the same as being loyal to and belonging to the 'people of God.' The criterion of belonging is the law, in Judaism, and the faith, in Christianity. A Jew is a person who keeps the laws, *shomer ha-mitzvôt*; a Christian is a person who believes in Christ. In the Christian perspective, both criteria are closely connected, because faith *(pistis)* in Christ is held to be the fulfillment, end, and goal *(telos)* of the law *(nomos)*. In both religions, the underlying idea is association with or dissociation from God and—at the same time—with or from his people. This is the general and normal structure of this type of religion. Under the condition of *Ernstfall*, in the frame of either covenantal or apocalyptic semantics, religion is susceptible to intensification up to the highest degree of total religion. In the Hebrew Bible, covenantal semantics prevails, but there are also foreshadowings of the apocalyptic form. In the New Testament, apocalypticism gains enormously in momentum, and in the Qur'an, the semantics of apocalypticism, the discourse of judgment, salvation and damnation, hell and paradise, as well as of God's friends and foes, is all-prevailing.[15] Given the challenge of globalization and the dangers of a world drifting toward a possible "clash of civilizations," it seems necessary not only to describe but to overcome the semantics of apocalypticism. It is with this "deconstructive" interest in mind that I am trying to trace this style of thought to its roots and origins. We have seen its first origins, still in the framework of covenant and the wrath of God, in the situation of Assyrian and Babylonian oppression, and have identified the conditions of its transformation and apocalyptic intensification in the time of Seleucid oppression that continued in the resistance against Rome.

To close, I would like to consider the role of writing or scripture in this context. According to a Jewish tradition, God sent down from heaven the book and the sword, *sefer ve-sayif.* The Maccabean opposition grasped the sword; the monotheist opposition in the seventh century BCE grasped the book. It produced a text that presents itself as the foundational document of the covenant, *sefer ha-b'rît* or *sefer hatorah*, giving rise to an unprecedented process of scriptural codification of the most varied normative and narrative traditions, leading eventually to the canon of the Hebrew Bible and, on the same model, the Christian Bible and the Qur'an. Writing—the concept of scripture or Holy Writ—seems to be a decisive factor in this connection of covenant, revelation, divine wrath, and holy zeal that we have tried to analyze with regard to the roots of religious violence.

The "book" also seems to be connected to the idea of *Ernstfall*. I am referring to the legend of the finding of the book as told in 2 Kings 22–23. Under King Josiah, during restoration work in the temple, a book is found that turns out to have been written by Moses himself, giving a summary of all the rules that must be observed in order to be allowed a blessed life in the Promised Land and announcing the most terrible punishments in case of abandonment. Since this book was forgotten and the rules neglected, catastrophe is inevitable. This situation fulfils exactly the definition of the religious *Ernstfall*. The crime is so general, and the imminent punishment so radical, that here the covenantal concept of *Ernstfall* in the form of the wrath of God assumes apocalyptic traits. To be sure, God does not reveal the end of the world and the imminent judgment, but only issues prescriptions, laws, and rules and insists on their codification, memorization, and observance. But the imminent punishment appears so terrible that under these conditions religion takes on another degree of intensification and assumes the traits of a total religion. All other spheres of culture are subordinated to religion and controlled by the law that forms the basis of the covenant: art by the prohibition of images, law and economy by corresponding regulations, cult by the ritual laws, and, above all, the political, the institution of kingship that is now clearly and completely subordinated under the Torah.

When the king ascends to the throne, we read in Deuteronomy 17,

> he shall write for himself a copy of this Torah in a book out of that which is before the priests, the Levites: And it shall be with him and he shall read therein all the days of his life : that he may learn to fear the LORD his God, to keep all the words of this Torah and these statutes, to do them: that his heart be not lifted up above his brethren, and that he turn not aside from this commandment, to the right hand or to the left: to the end that he may prolong his days in his kingdom, he, and his children, in the midst of Israel. (Deut. 17:18–20)

Kingship appears here as a more or less necessary evil whose dangers must be contained through scripture as effectively as possible. This, we might conclude, is total religion, not as a historical phenomenon in the time of Josiah, but as an idea arising in that time.

The notion of "total religion," to emphasize this point once again, does not refer to a specific religion, but to a degree of intensity that any religion that knows of revelation in the form of a codified will of God can assume, or various religious movements may proclaim. Examples of this impulse include the Maccabees and other *qana'im* in ancient Judaism, and Christianity during several phases of papal predominance in the Middle Ages, as well as puritan Protestant movements such as John Calvin's and Oliver Cromwell's theocratic institutions. Today, Islamist theocracies and movements confront us with similar manifestations of total religion.

This possibility of turning into a total religion seems to me to be the problem of monotheism. In the pagan world, something like total religion seems impossible. The so-called 'pagan religions' were centered on cult, and this cult was often violent and bloody. But they would not polarize people into friend and foe according to the criteria of an orthodoxy, whether of law or of faith. Wars were waged for reasons of greed or revenge or fear, but not for religious reasons. Ideas of an *Ernstfall* such as apocalypse and the Last Judgment were alien to these religions, and only the idea of an *Ernstfall*—in this I agree with Carl Schmitt—makes totalization possible, on the political as well as on the religious level.

Depoliticizing Religion

Let me emphasize two points of this reflection on the origins of religious violence. One is the connection between violence and *Ernstfall* as the condition under which the inevitable and everlasting dialectics and dynamics of association and dissociation, identity and difference, inclusion and exclusion turn into the distinction between friend and foe and thereby becomes a totalizing principle. Carl Schmitt discovered this connection in arguing for totalization, but one can also use his discovery in the opposite direction and argue for de-totalization, de-polarization, and de-politicization. This is what I am attempting to do here. In using Schmitt's theory, I am not following but contradicting him. I am following his analysis but drawing the opposite conclusions. What he wants to promote, I want to avoid and deconstruct.

The distinction between friend and foe belongs to the realm of politics; it has found its way into religion through the concept of the covenant that Israel adopted from Neo-Assyrian politics. This concept needed—and still needs—to be de-politicized and de-totalized. Jewish messianism was a step in this direction because it postponed the full political fulfillment of total religion at the end of history. Another anti-totalistic step was Jesus' teaching to "give back to Caesar what is Caesar's and to God what is God's" (Matt. 22:21; Mark 12:17; Luke 20:25), and also the statement "My kingdom is not of this world" (John 18:36). The Hebrew Bible is in any case safe from overly totalizing readings by virtue of the diversity of traditions that shaped it.

The other point to retain from this analysis is the connection of revelation and scripture. The Age of Enlightenment discovered a source of intolerance and violence in this alliance. This brings me to Lessing's and Mendelssohn's criticism of scripture.[16] Lessing relativized the authority of scripture against what he called the "spirit" of religion;[17] Mendelssohn relativized the authority of revelation by opposing it to nature and history. For Mendelssohn, Judaism is not a religion of "revelation" in the Christian sense of the word. "I believe," he writes in his essay *Jerusalem, oder Über religiöse Macht und Judentum* (Jerusalem, or, On Religious Power and Judaism, 1783), that "Judaism does not know of any revealed religion. The Israelites have laws, commandments, rules of life, instruction about the will of God . . . but no general doctrines, no salvific truths, no statements of universal reason. Those, God reveals to us always, in the same way as to all other people, through nature and history but never through language and writing."[18] In Jewish understanding, eternal truths are revealed to *all* mankind through the creation of the world, and they are—at least partially—readable by the reason with which God has equipped all human beings. They are a matter of reason and not of faith. They must never be codified in writing. "They were," Mendelssohn writes, "confided to the living, spiritual education that adapts to all the changes of times and circumstances."[19] Only "historical truths" must be written down, but never "eternal truths." The law that God gave or revealed to Moses on Mount Sinai is a kind of historical truth that could only survive by means of writing. "Only with regard to historical truths," Mendelssohn writes, "the Highest Wisdom deems it adequate to instruct human beings in human manner, i.e., by speech and writing."[20] The historical truth of the law concerns only the Jews; eternal truths concern the whole of humanity. Truths of reason are "*allgemeine Menschenreligion* [the general religion of mankind], not Judaism, and general human religion . . . was not to be revealed on Mount Sinai. Judaism does not boast of any exclusive revelation of eternal truths, of no revealed religion in the general [i.e., the Christian] use of the term."[21] What Mendelssohn is opposing could perhaps be called the 'absolutism of difference,' which he detects as a dangerous consequence in the Christian idea of revelation. He presents the Jewish concept of revelation as a counterexample that avoids the absolutism of difference by claiming only local or particular validity, thus allowing integration into, or subordination under, the overarching concept of *Menschenreligion*. For Mendelssohn, *Menschenreligion* is synonymous with 'natural religion.' Whereas natural religion was generally taken as the irreconcilable opposite of revealed religion, Mendelssohn understands them as complementary concepts. All humans live in a status of double membership, belonging both to their particular religion and to general human religion, the one transmitted to them by scriptural and oral tradition, the other revealed to them by reason, attention, and contemplation.

Lessing opposes the absolutism of difference on a much broader scale in his "Masonic dialogues" *Ernst und Falk*. Besides the religious difference, which he, like Mendelssohn, attributes to a mistaken concept of revelation, he also addresses political and social differences that negate, destroy, and preclude the unity of mankind, the idea of humanity. Lessing's concept of a cosmopolitanism that overcomes the barriers of religion, nation, and class, and Mendelssohn's concept of *Menschenreligion*, the religion of mankind, both relate to the idea of 'humanity' in the sense of a trans-religious, trans-confessional, transnational, and trans-hierarchical system of values, needs, and properties to which all human beings aspire, apart from membership in their specific religion, nation, and class. This overarching level of the unity of humanity breaks the absolutism of difference which precludes tolerance and mutual understanding.

With the idea of humanity, we have come full circle: on the opposite side from Carl Schmitt, with whom we started. "Whoever speaks of humanity," Schmitt states laconically, "wants to deceive."[22] For Schmitt, humanity or mankind does not exist because it excludes the other, the enemy. "If the distinction between friend and foe vanishes, even as a pure possibility," he writes, "all that still exists after this event is de-politicized Weltanschauung, culture, civilization, economy, morality, law, art, entertainment, etc., but no state, no politics. Humankind as such is unable to wage war, for it has no enemy, at least not on this planet. The concept 'humanity' excludes the concept of enmity."[23] With these words, Schmitt reveals himself as a partisan of what I have called "the absolutism of difference" and as an enemy of any form of "double membership." His arch enemies are the

Freemasons, the cosmopolitans, and above all the Jews. Schmitt is the most pronounced exponent of what Thomas Mann has called "the new world of anti-humanism" *(Anti-Humanität)*.[24] With the same intensity with which Thomas Mann abhorred "anti-humanity," Schmitt abhorred the idea of humanity because it would destroy all distinctions and differences, above all the distinction between friend and foe, the basis not only for political identity but for identity as such.

This last argument, however, is nonsense or propaganda. The concept of humanity excludes neither nationality nor enmity. The natural enemy of the cosmopolitan is not the inhabitant of another planet, as Schmitt assumed, but the unconditional particularist, be it in the sense of nationalism, racism, or religious fundamentalism. The concept of humanity does not exclude difference, but the absolutism of difference.

The concept of humanity is frequently denounced as a western concept and as mere imperialism in disguise. Whether or not the idea is of western origin, however, is immaterial. What counts is that it is aspired to by east and west, north and south. As soon as the concept of *humanitas* and its values are globally claimed, they cease to be western or eastern and become universal. It is not the origin but the goal that matters.

Unlike Mendelssohn, we would perhaps not speak of religion—*Menschheitsreligion*, the religion of humanity—with respect to the idea of *humanitas*. Instead—and more modestly—we could perhaps speak of a "global civility." This idea should be understood in purely secular terms. In the course of globalization, we are moving toward a kind of world society, but not toward a world religion in the sense of the eighteenth century. There will never be one religion on earth and there will never be any agreement about God—at least before the messianic age. Until then, religion exists only in the plural. Agreement about global civility cannot be based on God and revelation, but on reason and insight. These, however, should not be opposites. The existing religions can easily adopt these principles, and to the degree that they do so, they cease to be agents of polarization and start working as agents of humanization. The less specifically religious the idea of a global civility—human rights and what this idea implies—is, the easier it is for the various religions to lend it support. Violence belongs to the realm not of religion but of politics. Religion appears to be the only power that is strong enough to confront politics, to overcome violence, and to promote peace, understanding, and justice.

NOTES

Notes to Chapter 1

1   "Ägyptischer Totenglaube im Rahmen der Struktur ägyptischer Religion," in *Eranos Jahrbuch* (1965 [1967]), 399–446. Cf. Siegfried Morenz, *Gott und Mensch im Alten Ägypten* (Leipzig: Koehler und Amelang, 1964), 19ff.

2   For a critical assessment of this distinction, introduced by Theo Sundermeier, see Andreas Wagner, ed., *Primäre und sekundäre Religion als Kategorie der Religionsgeschichte des Alten Testaments* (Berlin and New York: de Gruyter, 2006). For the classification of ancient Egypt as a 'primary religion' see Jan Assmann, "Kulte und Religionen: Merkmale primärer und sekundärer Religion(serfahrung) im Alten Ägypten," in Wagner, *Primäre und sekundäre Religion*, 269–88.

3   For a somewhat different but comparable approach see Martin Riesebrodt, *Cultus und Heilsversprechen: Eine Theorie der Religionen* (Munich: C.H. Beck, 2007).

4   The Latin term used by Cicero and others to describe the aims of religion, *placatio deorum* ('appeasing the gods'), corresponds exactly to the Egyptian term *se-hetep netjeru*.

5   See Jan Assmann, *Death and Salvation in Ancient Egypt*, translated by David Lorton (Ithaca, NY: Cornell University Press, 2005), chapter 15.

6   In his book *De la divinité du pharaon* (Paris: Imprimerie nationale, 1960), Georges Posener warns against overstressing the divinity of pharaoh in ancient Egypt, adducing several texts where the king appears in a human and often even all-too-human light. These texts belong to secular literature, showing the king not in his official and cultic roles, but as a person. The divinity of the king, however, is a matter of role and not of personal charisma.

7   See Jan Assmann, *Der König als Sonnenpriester* (Glückstadt: J.J. Augustin, 1971), translated as *Egyptian Solar Religion in the New Kingdom* by Anthony Alcock (London: Kegan Paul International, 1995), chapter 1.

8   For the funerary rites see John H. Taylor, *Death and the Afterlife in Ancient Egypt* (London: British Museum Press, 2000) and Assmann, *Death and Salvation in Ancient Egypt*.

9   For details, see Jan Assmann, *The Search for God in Ancient Egypt*, translated by David Lorton (Ithaca, NY: Cornell University Press, 2001).

10 The extant manuscripts date from the late Eighteenth Dynasty, and Andrea Loprieno-Gnirs advocates such a late date even for the text itself: "Das Motiv des Bürgerkriegs in 'Merikare und Neferti': Zur Literatur der 18. Dynastie," in *Jn.t.dr.w: Festschrift für Friedrich Junge*, edited by Gerald Moers, 207–65 (Göttingen: Seminar für Ägyptologie und Koptologie, 2006).

11 Merikare P 130–38, in Aksel Volten, *Zwei altägyptische politische Schriften: Die Lehre für König Merikarê* (Analecta Aegyptiaca 4. Copenhagen: E. Munksgaard, 1945), 73–78.

12 Georges Posener, "Sur le monothéisme dans l'ancienne Égypte," in *Mélanges bibliques et orientaux en l'honneur de M. Henri Gazelles*, edited by A. Caquot and M. Delcor (Alter Orient und Altes Testament 212. Kevelaer, Germany: Butzon & Bercker, 1981), 347–51.

13 For the question of poly-, mono-, and henotheism in ancient Egypt see the magisterial study by Erik Hornung, *Conceptions of God in Ancient Egypt: The One and the Many*, translated by John Baines (Ithaca, NY: Cornell University Press, 1982).

14 pBoulaq 17 = pCairo CG 58038, iv, 3–5; cf. Assmann, *Egyptian Solar Religion*, 125. See also Merikare 130–38, in Assmann, *Egyptian Solar Religion*, 119f.; Jan Assmann, *Ma'at: Gerechtigkeit und Unsterblichkeit im alten Ägypten* (Munich: C.H. Beck, 1990), 234f.

15 Eric Voegelin, *Order and History 1: Israel and Revelation* (Baton Rouge: University of Louisiana Press, 1956), 8.

16 See Erik Hornung, *Echnaton: Die Religion des Lichts* (Zürich: Artemis, 2005; translated as *Akhenaten and the Religion of Light* by David Lorton (Ithaca, NY, and London: Cornell University Press, 1999).

17 Jan Zandee, "De Hymnen aan Amon van Pap. Leiden I 350," *Oudheidkundige Mededelingen van het Rijksmuseum van Oudheiden te Leiden* 28 (1947): 20–21, pl. iv; Jan Assmann, *Ägyptische Hymnen und Gebete* (=*ÄHG*) 139 (Zurich: Artemis, 1975).

18 Zandee, "Hymnen," 75–86; *ÄHG* 138.

19   Cf. Jan Assmann, "Theological Responses to Amarna," in *Egypt, Israel, and the Ancient Mediterranean World: Studies in Honor of Donald B. Redford*, edited by Gary N. Knoppers and Antoine Hirsch (Cologne and Leiden: Brill, 2004), 179–91.

20   See Assmann, *Egyptian Solar Religion*, chapters 1 and 2.

21   See Assmann, *Egyptian Solar Religion*, chapter 3.

22   Leiden V 70 = *ÄHG* no. 90; Leiden K 11 = Kenneth A. Kitchen, *Ramesside Inscriptions Historical and Biographical*, vol. 3 (Oxford, UK: Blackwell, 1969), 175, ll. 2–5.

23   Maj Sandman, ed., *Texts from the Time of Akhenaten* (Bibliotheca Aegyptiaca 8. Brussels: Fondation Reine Élizabeth, 1938), 95, ll. 12–13. On this passage cf. Gerhard Fecht, "Zur Frühform der Amarna-Theologie: Neubearbeitung der Stele der Architekten Suti und Hor," *Zeitschrift für Ägyptische Sprache* 94 (1967): 33; Jan Assmann, *Sonnenhymnen in Thebanischen Gräbern* (= *STG*. Theben 1. Mainz: Philipp von Zabern, 1983), Text 54 (x).

24   Sandman, *Texts*, 15, 1–9; cf. Assmann, *STG*, Text 253(s).

25   Zandee, "Hymnen," 75–86; Assmann, *ÄHG* 318, no. 138.

26   On the concept of the "limitlessness" of god, see the phrase "who concealed himself, whose limits cannot be attained," pLeiden I 344 verso ii, 8–9, in Jan Zandee, *Der Amunshymnus des Papyrus Leiden I 344, Verso* (Leiden: Brill, 1992), 120–26. See also pBerlin 3049, 16, 6 (Assmann, *ÄHG* 278, no. 127A, verse 113) and Kurt Sethe, *Thebanische Tempelinschriften aus griechisch-römischerer Zeit*, edited by Otto Firchow (Urkunden des aegyptischen Altertums 8. Berlin: Akademie-Verlag, 1957), 116: "whose circuit has no limits."

27   Papyrus Mag. Harris IV, 1–2 = Hibis 32,1, *ÄHG* Nr. 129, 1–6.

28   pLeiden I 344 verso. III, 2–3 = Zandee, *Der Amunshymnus*, 168–76.

29   Emile Chassinat, *Le temple d'Edfou*, vol. 3 (Cairo: Imprimerie de l'Institut français d'archéologie orientale, 1928), 34.9–10.

30   ḥprw m ḥḥw: stela of Ramesses III = Kenneth A. Kitchen, *Ramesside Inscriptions Historical and Biographical*, vol. 6 (Oxford, UK: Blackwell, 1969), 452.8.

31   Sethe, *Thebanische Tempelinschriften*, §138b, p. 110. Of Yahweh, on the contrary, it is said: "'One' is his name" (Zechariah 14:9).

32   Serge Sauneron, ed., *Le papyrus magique illustré de Brooklyn* (Wilbour Monographs 3. New York: The Brooklyn Museum, 1970), 23, and pl. IV, fig. 3 (facing p. 13).

33   Assmann, *STG*, 124f.

34   See A.J. Festugière, *La révélation d'Hermès Trismégiste 2: Le dieu cosmique* (Paris: Les Belles Lettres, 1949), who, however, ignores the Egyptian

background of this conception and derives Hermetic theology only from Greek origins. For Egyptian connections see Jan Assmann, *Moses the Egyptian: The Memory of Egypt in Western Monotheism* (Cambridge, MA: Harvard University Press, 1997), chapter 6.

35 Reinhold Merkelbach and Maria Totti, eds., *Abrasax: Ausgewählte Papyri religiösen und magischen Inhalts*, vol. 1 (Opladen, Germany: Westdeutscher Verlag, 1990), 136f. See pages 127–34 of the same book for similar Greek texts and their striking parallels with Ramesside theology.

36 For the history of this formula see Assmann, *Moses the Egyptian*, 204–207.

37 *Te tibi, una quae es omnia, dea Isis, Arrius Balbinus v(oti) c(ompos)*: "Arrius Balbinus dedicates you [i.e., your statue] to you, goddess Isis, who being One are All, for my wish is fulfilled"; after Reinhold Merkelbach, *Isis Regina, Zeus Sarapis: Die griechisch-ägyptische Religion nach den Quellen dargestellt* (Stuttgart: B. Teubner, 1995), 98.

38 Macrobius, *Saturnalia* I 20, 16–17, cited in R. van den Broek, "The Sarapis Oracle in Macrobius, *Saturnalia* I 20, 16–17," in *Hommages à Maarten J. Vermaseren* (EPRO 68.1. Leiden: Brill, 1978), 123–41; Merkelbach, *Isis Regina*, 129f.

39 Ptahhotep, pPrisse 6, 5; see Gerhard Fecht, *Der Habgierige und die Maat in der Lehre des Ptahhotep* (Glückstadt; J.J. Augustin, 1958), 11–34.

40 See Assmann, *Death and Salvation*, especially chapters 3, 16, and 17.

41 *Instructions for Merikare* P 53–57, translated by Joachim Friedrich Quack, *Studien zur Lehre für Merikare* (Göttinger Orientforschungen 23. Wiesbaden: Harrassowitz, 1992), 34f.

42 Alexandre Varille, "L'inscription du mystique Baki," *Bulletin de l'Institut français d'archéologie orientale* 54 (1954): 129–35; Assmann, *Ma'at*, 134–36; Miriam Lichtheim, *Maat in Egyptian Autobiographies and Related Studies* (Orbis Biblicus et Orientalis 120. Fribourg, Switzerland: Universitätsverlag, 1992), 103–105, 127–33.

43 For this understanding of personal piety see Assmann, *Egyptian Solar Religion*, chapter 7, and Assmann, *The Search for God in Ancient Egypt*, chapter 9. In a more general sense, personal piety is a structural and metahistorical element of religion which even in Egypt was certainly not restricted to the Ramesside period: see John Baines, "Society, Morality, and Religious Practice," in *Religion in Ancient Egypt: Gods, Myths, and Personal Practice*, edited by Byron E. Shafer (Ithaca: Cornell University Press, 1991), 123–200, and "Practical Religion and Piety," *Journal of Egyptian Archaeology* 73 (1987): 79–98. I am using the term following the lead of James Henry Breasted, who seems to have invented it in his *Development of Religion and Thought in Ancient Egypt* (1912) with respect

to a religious movement that made its first appearance, as Georges Posener has shown, in the context of Theban feasts in the time of Thutmose III and Amenophis II ("La piété personnelle avant l'âge amarnien," *Revue d'Égyptologie* 27 (1975): 195–210) and came to full fruition after the breakdown of the Amarna movement.

44 See the references in Jan Assmann, *Zeit und Ewigkeit im alten Ägypten: Ein Beitrag zur Geschichte der Ewigkeit* (Abhandlungen der Heidelberger Akademie der Wissenschaften, Philosophisch-Historische Klasse 1975, 66. Heidelberg: C. Winter, 1975).

Notes to Chapter 2

1 In Judaism, the first night of the week of Pesach (Passover) is devoted to a celebration of the Exodus called "Seder" (lit. 'order').

2 "Der Ausgang des Menschen aus seiner selbstverschuldeten Unmündigkeit": Kant's famous definition of the concept of *Aufklärung* ('enlightenment'). See Immanuel Kant, "Beantwortung der Frage: Was ist Aufklärung?" *Berlinische Monatsschrift* 4 (1784): 481–94.

3 For a less skeptical treatment see James K. Hoffmeier, *Israel in Egypt: The Evidence for the Authenticity of the Exodus Tradition* (New York: Oxford University Press, 1997).

4 Cicero, *De inventione*, 1, 34–1, 43, cited in Thomas Aquinas, *Summa Theologica* I–II q7 a3 c.

5 Donald B. Redford, *Egypt, Canaan, and Israel in Ancient Times* (Princeton: Princeton University Press, 1992), 98–122, 408–29. Flavius Josephus identified the report of the expulsion of the Hyksos in Manetho's *Aigyptiaka* with the Exodus of the Israelites in his *Contra Apionem* I, 14–15 §§73–105 and I, 26–31 §§227–87.

6 See chapter 1.

7 Redford, *Egypt*, 170ff., 195.

8 Tursha = Tyrrhenians; Shekelesh = Sicily; Shardana = Sardinia; Ekwesh = Achaioi, Acheans; Lukka = Lycia; Peleset = Philistines, Palestine.

9 Morton Smith, *Palestinian Parties and Politics that Shaped the Old Testament* (New York and London: Columbia University Press, 1971).

10 I am following a revised form of the "Documentary Hypothesis," which discerns several sources and textual strata in the composition of the Biblical text, but assumes a closed composition for the basic text comprising the books of Genesis and Exodus as a work of the priestly school (P^G), into which earlier sources, such as the "Yahwist," the "Book of the Covenant" (*sefer ha-b'rit*), and others are integrated. This book was later amplified by additions. I will not enter into fruitless discussions with

commentators who still believe not only in the historicity of the Exodus but also in the authorship of Moses; see, for example, Douglas K. Stuart, *Exodus* (The New American Commentary 2. Nashville, TN: Broadman & Holman, 2006).

11 George E. Mendenhall, *Law and Covenant in Israel and the Ancient Near East* (Pittsburgh: The Biblical Colloquium, 1955); Klaus Baltzer, *The Covenant Formulary: In Old Testament, Jewish and Early Christian Writings*, translated by David E. Green (Philadelphia: Fortress, 1971); Dennis J. McCarthy, *Treaty and Covenant: A Study in Form in the Ancient Oriental Documents and in the Old Testament*, 2nd ed. (Analecta Biblica 21. Rome: Biblical Institute Press, 1978).

12 Alan Dundes, *The Morphology of North American Indian Folk Tales* (Folklore Fellows Communications 195. Helsinki: Suomalainen Tiedeakatamie, 1964.)

13 See Nahum B. Sarna, *Exploring Exodus: The Origins of Biblical Israel* (New York: Socken Books, 1986), 76.

14 See Peter Der Manuelian, *Living in the Past: Studies in Archaism of the Egyptian Twenty-sixth Dynasty* (London: Kegan Paul International, 1994), and Jan Assmann, *The Mind of Egypt: History and Meaning in the Time of the Pharaohs*, translated by Andrew Jenkins (New York: Metropolitan Books, 2002), 335–64.

15 Stefan M. Maul, "Altertum in Mesopotamien: Beiträge zu den Sektions-themen und Diskussionen," in *Die Gegenwart des Altertums: Formen und Funktionen des Altertumsbezugs in den Hochkulturen der Alten Welt*, edited by Dieter Kuhn and Helga Stahl (Heidelberg: Edition Forum, 2001), 117–24; Gerdien Jonker, *The Topography of Remembrance: The Dead, Tradition, and Collective Memory in Mesopotamia* (Leiden: E.J. Brill, 1995).

16 Translated by Jan Assmann from Eckart Otto, *Das Deuteronomium: Politische Theologie und Rechtsreform in Juda und Assyrien* (Berlin: de Gruyter, 1999), 82.

17 Cf. Jan Assmann, *Cultural Memory and Early Civilization: Writing, Remembrance, and Political Imagination* (New York: Cambridge University Press, 2011), 191–205.

18 Cf. Deut. 6:7: "and shalt talk of them when thou sittest in thine house, and when thou walkest by the way, and when thou liest down, and when thou risest up."

19 Deut. 13:1 in the Hebrew verse numbering; Deut. 12:32 in the Authorized Version of the Bible.

20 Exodus 12:1–17.

21 This discussion is based on *Hagadah shel Pesah: The Passover Haggadah*, translated and commented by Rabbi Joseph Elias (New York: Mesorah Publications, 2000).

22 In the *New York Times* of 22 March 2002, the Jewish periodical *Tikkun* had an advertisement, recommending "to turn part of your Passover Seder into a mini teach-in about the way that Israel is increasingly perceived as Pharaoh to a population that is seeking its freedom and self-determination," continuing with the phrase quoted above.

23 *Passover Haggadah*, 148f.

24 Erving Goffman, *Frame Analysis: An Essay on the Organization of Experience* (New York: Harper and Row, 1974).

25 *Passover Haggadah*, 56f.

26 *Passover Haggadah*, 70–77.

27 *Passover Haggadah*, 46f. Cf. Siegfried Stein, "The Influence of Symposium Literature on the Literary Form of the Pesah Haggadah," *Journal of Jewish Studies* 8 (1957): 13–44.

28 Hoffmeier, *Israel in Egypt*.

29 *Passover Haggadah*, 126–35.

30 *Passover Haggadah*, 214f.

31 The French and German names for a mythical land of plenty, a frequent literary theme in medieval Europe.

32 Michael Walzer, *Exodus and Revolution* (New York: Basic Books, 1985).

33 For the identification of Scotland and England with Biblical Israel in the times of the Reformation and the Civil War see Andreas Pečar, *Macht der Schrift: Politischer Biblizismus in Schottland und England zwischen Reformation und Bürgerkrieg (1534–1642)* (Munich: R. Oldenbourg Verlag, 2011).

34 See chapter 1, note 2.

35 'Crush the infamous,' a phrase frequently used by Voltaire in response to abuses of the people by royalty and the clergy in France.

Notes to Chapter 3

1 See Jacques Derrida, *Limited Inc.* (Evanston, IL: Northwestern University Press, 1988).

2 See Volker Gerhardt, Klaus Lucas, and Günter Stock, eds., *Evolution: Theorie, Formen und Konsequenzen eines Paradigmas in Natur, Technik und Kultur* (Berlin: Akademie Verlag, 2011).

3 The idea of the three ages goes back to the "Apokryphon Eliae," which is of great importance for Luther's concept of sacred history and which is even quoted in the Talmud as a prophecy of Elijah (bSanh 97ab, Aboda

zara 9a): two thousand years before the Torah, two thousand years under the Torah, two thousand years of messianic time.

4   Cf. Jacob Taubes, *Abendländische Eschatologie* (Bern: A. Francke, 1947; 2nd ed. Berlin: Matthes & Seitz, 2007); translated into English as *Occidental Eschatology* (Stanford, CA: Stanford University Press, 2009).

5   See Karl Löwith, *Meaning in History: The Theological Implications of the Philosophy of History* (Chicago: University of Chicago Press, 1949); Amos Funkenstein, *Heilsplan und natürliche Entwicklung: Formen der Gegenwartsbestimmung im Geschichtsdenken des hohen Mittelalters* (Munich: Nymphenburger Verlagshandlung, 1965).

6   For Jewish adaptations of the theory of divine accommodation see S.D. Benin, "The Cunning of God and Divine Accommodation," *Journal of the History of Ideas* 45 (1984): 179–92.

7   Sigmund Freud, *Moses and Monotheism*, translated by James Strachey (The Standard Edition of the Complete Psychological Works of Sigmund Freud 23. London: Hogarth Press, 1953–74).

8   In the sense of Niklas Luhmann, *Ideenevolution: Beiträge zur Wissenssoziologie* (Frankfurt am Main: Suhrkamp, 2008).

9   The first to use the metaphors of matrimony and love, adultery and jealousy, in order to express the singular relationship between Yahweh and Israel is the prophet Hosea, active in the Northern Kingdom in the late eighth century BCE. He is also the first to allude to the myth of the Exodus.

10 George E. Mendenhall, *Law and Covenant in Israel and the Ancient Near East* (Pittsburgh: Biblical Colloquium, 1955); Klaus Baltzer, *The Covenant Formulary: In Old Testament, Jewish and Early Christian Writings*, translated by David E. Green (Philadelphia: Fortress, 1971); Dennis J. McCarthy, *Treaty and Covenant: A Study in Form in the Ancient Oriental Documents and in the Old Testament*, 2nd ed. (Analecta Biblica 21. Rome: Biblical Institute Press, 1978).

11 Eckart Otto, *Das Deuteronomium: Politische Theologie und Rechtsreform in Juda und Assyrien* (Berlin: de Gruyter, 1999); Hans Ulrich Steymans, *Deuteronomium 28 und die adê zur Thronfolgeregelung Asarhaddons: Segen und Fluch im Alten Orient und in Israel* (Fribourg, Switzerland and Göttingen: Universitätsverlag, 1995).

12 See esp. Morton Smith, *Palestinian Parties and Politics that Shaped the Old Testament* (New York and London: Columbia University Press, 1971).

13 Benjamin Nelson, *The Idea of Usury: From Tribal Brotherhood to Universal Otherhood* (Princeton: Princeton University Press, 1949).

14 See Jan Assmann, *Ägyptische Hymnen und Gebete (ÄHG)*, 2nd ed. (Fribourg, Switzerland: Universitätsverlag; Göttingen: Vandenhoeck & Ruprecht, 1999).

15 pBoulaq 17= pCairo CG 58038, iv, 3–5, *ÄHG* No. 87C. See also chapter 1, where this text is quoted at greater length.

16 *ÄHG* No. 92, 83–104.

17 "O sole god, beside whom there is none!" Maj Sandman, *Texts from the Time of Akhenaten* (Bibliotheca Aegyptiaca 8. Brussels: Fondation Reine Élisabeth, 1938), 94, 17; cf. "There is no other except him," Sandman, 7, 7–8.

18 C.S. Lewis, *The Allegory of Love: A Study in Medieval Tradition* (New York: Oxford University Press, 1958), 57.

Notes to Chapter 4

1 Carl Richard Lepsius, *Über den ersten ägyptischen Götterkreis und seine geschichtlich-mythologische Entstehung* (Berlin: Abhandlungen der Akademie der Wissenschaften, 1851), 40; translated by Jan Assmann.

2 Sigmund Freud, *Der Mann Moses und die monotheistische Religion* (Amsterdam: De Lange, 1939; English translation by James Strachey, *Moses and Monotheism* (The Standard Edition of the Complete Psychological Works of Sigmund Freud 23. London: Hogarth Press, 1964) (= SE), 1–137.

3 *The Letters of Sigmund Freud and Arnold Zweig*, translated by W.D. Robson-Scott (London: Hogarth Press, 1970), 91.

4 See Jan Assmann, "Akhanyati's Theology of Light and Time," *Proceedings of the Israel Academy of Sciences and Humanities* 7, no. 4 (1992): 143–76.

5 Ernst Sellin, *Mose und seine Bedeutung für die israelitisch-jüdische Religionsgeschichte* (Erlangen and Leipzig: Deichert, 1922).

6 Sellin, *Mose und seine Bedeutung*, 73–113.

7 Klaus Baltzer, *Kommentar zum Alten Testament: Deutero-Jesaja* (Gütersloh: Gütersloher Verlagshaus, 1999); Ellen Bradshaw Aitken, *Jesus' Death in Early Christian Memory: The Poetics of the Passion* (Göttingen: Vandenhoeck & Ruprecht, 2004).

8 Freud, *Moses and Monotheism*, 80.

9 Freud, *Moses and Monotheism*, 80.

10 Freud, *Moses and Monotheism*, 101.

11 Yosef Hayim Yerushalmi, *Freud's Moses: Judaism Terminable and Interminable* (New Haven: Yale University Press, 1991).

12 Freud, *Moses and Monotheism*, 99.

13 Freud, *Moses and Monotheism*, 100.

14 Aleida Assmann, "Impact and Resonance: Towards a Theory of Emotions in Cultural Memory." Lecture held at Södertörn University, 18 May 2011. Södertörn Lectures 6. Huddinge, Sweden: Södertörn University, 2012.

15 Jan Assmann, *Re und Amun: Die Krise des polytheistischen Weltbilds im Ägypten der 18.–20. Dynastie* (Orbis Biblicus et Orientalis 51. Fribourg,

Switzerland and Göttingen: Universitätsverlag, 1983); translated by Anthony Alcock as *Egyptian Solar Religion in the New Kingdom: Re, Amun, and the Crisis of Polytheism* (London: Kegan Paul International, 1995).

16 James P. Allen, "The Natural Philosophy of Akhenaten," in *Religion and Philosophy in Ancient Egypt*, edited by W.K. Simpson (Yale Egyptological Studies 3. New Haven: Yale University Press, 1989), 89–101.

17 Assmann, "Akhanyati's Theology of Light and Time," n. 4.

18 Eckart Otto, *Das Deuteronomium: Politische Theologie und Rechtsreform in Juda und Assyrien* (Berlin: de Gruyter, 1999); Hans Ulrich Steymans, *Deuteronomium 28 und die adê zur Thronfolgeregelung Asarhaddons: Segen und Fluch im Alten Orient und in Israel* (Fribourg, Switzerland and Göttingen: Universitätsverlag, 1995).

19 See Jan Assmann, "Ocular Desire in a Time of Darkness: Urban Festivals and Divine Visibility in Ancient Egypt," *Torat ha-Adam (Jahrbuch für religiöse Anthropologie/Yearbook of Religious Anthropology)* 1 (1994): 13–29.

20 Hans Goedicke, "The 'Canaanite Illness,'" *Studien zur Altägyptischen Kultur* 11 (1984): 91–105; Goedicke, "The End of the Hyksos in Egypt," *Egyptological Studies in Honor of Richard A. Parker*, edited by Leonard H. Lesko (Hanover and London: University Press of New England, 1986), 37–47.

21 Wolfgang Helck, *Urkunden der 18. Dynastie*, Heft 22 (Berlin: Akademieverlag, 1958), 2025f.; translated by Jan Assmann. See Marc Gabolde, "Ay, Toutankhamoun et les Martelages de la Stèle de la Restauration de Karnak (CG 34183)," *Bulletin de la Société d'Égyptologie, Genève* 11 (1987): 37–61.

22 "Neferti," edited by Wolfgang Helck, *Die Prophezeiung des Neferti* (Wiesbaden: O. Harrassowitz, 1970), 46f.

23 Aleida Assmann, "Impact and Resonance," n. 109.

24 Gabrielle M. Spiegel, "Memory and History: Liturgical Time and Historical Time," *History and Theory* 41 (2002): 149–62.

25 Flavius Josephus, *Contra Apionem* I, 26–31 §§ 227–87 = Manetho Fr. 54, in *Manetho*, edited and translated by W.G. Waddell (Loeb Classical Library. Cambridge, MA: Harvard University Press, 1940), 118–47.

26 Waddell, *Manetho*, 120–23.

27 See Dietrich Wildung, *Egyptian Saints: Deification in Pharaonic Egypt* (New York: New York University Press, 1977).

28 Waddell, *Manetho*, §248, p. 130f.

29 Waddell, *Manetho*, §250, p. 130f.

30 Waddell, *Manetho*, §229, p. 120f.

31 Eduard Meyer, *Aegyptische Chronologie* (Abhandlungen der Preussischen Akademie der Wissenschaften. Leipzig: Verlag der Königlichen Akademie der Wissenschaften, 1904), 92–95.

32   Jan Assmann, *Ägypten: Theologie und Frömmigkeit einer frühen Hochkultur* (Stuttgart: Kohlhammer, 1984), 258–67; translated by David Lorton as *The Search for God in Ancient Egypt* (Ithaca, NY: Cornell University Press, 2001), 221–30.

33   Jan Assmann, "Ancient Egyptian Antijudaism: A Case of Distorted Memory," in *Memory Distortion: How Minds, Brains, and Societies Reconstruct the Past*, edited by D.L. Shacter, J.T. Coyle, G.D. Fischbach, M.M. Mesulam, and L.E. Sullivan (Cambridge, MA: Harvard University Press, 1996), 365–76.

34   Kim Ryholt, "Egyptian Historical Literature from the Greco-Roman Period," in *Das Ereignis: Geschichtsschreibung zwischen Vorfall und Befund*, edited by Martin Fitzenreiter (IBAES 10. London: Golden House Publications, 2009), 231–38, esp. 236f.

35   See below, p. 77.

36   Siegfried Schott, ed., *Urkunden mythologischen Inhalts* (Leipzig: J.C. Hinrichs, 1929), 17.22–18.13, translated by Jan Assmann; the entire list of Seth's religious crimes continues to 25.2. See Jan Assmann, *The Mind of Egypt: History and Meaning in the Time of the Pharaohs*, translated by Andrew Jenkins (New York: Cambridge University Press, 2002), 390–93.

37   Karl Theodor Zauzich, "Das Lamm des Bokchoris," in *Papyrus Erzherzog Rainer: Festschrift zum 100-jährigen Bestehen der Papyrussammlung der Oesterreichischen Nationalbibliothek* (Vienna: Brüder Hollinek, 1983), 165–74, translated by Jan Assmann; Zauzich, "Lamm des Bokchoris," in *Lexikon der Ägyptologie* III (Wiesbaden, 1980), 912f.; Donald B. Redford, *Pharaonic King-Lists, Annals, and Day-Books: A Contribution to the Study of the Egyptian Sense of History* (Mississauga: Benben, 1986), 286f.

38   "And let them make me a sanctuary; that I may dwell among them" (Exod. 25:8). "And I will meet there with the sons of Israel, and it shall be consecrated by My glory. And I will consecrate the tent of meeting and the altar; I will also consecrate Aaron and his sons to minister as priests to Me. And I will dwell among the sons of Israel and will be their God. And they shall know that I am the LORD their God who brought them out of the land of Egypt, that I might dwell among them; I am the LORD their God" (Exod. 29:43–46). "Moreover, I will make My dwelling among you, and My soul will not reject you. I will also walk among you and be your God, and you shall be My people. I am the LORD your God, who brought you out of the land of Egypt so that you should not be their slaves, and I broke the bars of your yoke and made you walk erect" (Lev. 26:11–13). "And you shall not defile the land in which you live, in the midst of which I dwell; for I the LORD am dwelling in the midst of the sons of Israel" (Num. 35:34).

39 *Corpus Hermeticum: Asclepius,* edited by A.D. Nock, translated by A.-J. Festugière (Paris: Collection Budé, Les Belles Lettres, 1945), 326–29. Coptic version: Martin Krause and Pahor Labib, eds., *Gnostische und hermetische Schriften aus Codex II und Codex VI,* 8.65.15–78.43 (Glückstadt: Augustin, 1971), 194–200. Cf. G. Fowden, *The Egyptian Hermes: A Historical Approach to the Late Pagan Mind* (Cambridge and New York: Cambridge University Press, 1986), 39–43; Jean-Pierre Mahé, *Hermès en Haute-Égypte,* vol. 2 (Quebec: Presses de l'Université Laval, 1978), 69–97.

Notes to Chapter 5

1 Karl Jaspers, *Vom Ursprung und Ziel der Geschichte* (Munich: Piper, 1949). See S.N. Eisenstadt, ed., *The Origins and Diversity of Axial Age Civilizations* (Albany: State University of New York Press, 1986); Benjamin Schwartz, *Wisdom, Revelation, and Doubt: Perspectives on the First Millennium B.C.* (Daedalus 104, 2. Boston: American Academy of Arts and Sciences, 1975); S.N. Eisenstadt, ed., *Kulturen der Achsenzeit. Ihre Ursprünge und ihre Vielfalt,* 2 vols. (Frankfurt: Suhrkamp, 1987); S.N. Eisenstadt, ed., *Kulturen der Achsenzeit II. Ihre institutionelle und kulturelle Dynamik,* 3 vols. (Frankfurt am Main: Suhrkamp, 1992); Johann P. Arnason, S.N. Eisenstadt, and Björn Wittrock, eds., *Axial Civilizations and World History* (Leiden: Brill, 2005); Robert Bellah and Hans Joas, eds., *The Axial Age and Its Consequences* (Cambridge, MA: Harvard University Press, 2012).

2 Jaspers, *Vom Ursprung,* 19. This and the subsequent translations of Jaspers are by Jan Assmann.

3 Jaspers, *Vom Ursprung,* 20f.

4 Jaspers, *Vom Ursprung,* 29f.

5 See Aleida and Jan Assmann, "Einleitung: Schrift—Kognition—Evolution. Eric A. Havelock und die Technologie kultureller Kommunikation," in E.A. Havelock, *Die Schriftrevolution im antiken Griechenland* (Weinheim: VCH Publications, 1990), 1–36. On pp. 27–28, we give a bibliography of the works published by Ong, Goody, and Havelock until 1990.

6 See Dieter Metzler, "A.H. Anquetil-Duperron (1731–1805) und das Konzept der Achsenzeit," *Achaemenid History* 7 (1991): 123–33; Dieter Metzler, *Kleine Schriften zur Geschichte und Religion des Altertums und deren Nachleben* (Münster: Ugarit-Verlag, 2004), 565 ff. and 577 ff.

7 Alan Henderson Gardiner, ed., *The Admonitions of an Egyptian Sage,* Tablet BM 5645 rto. 2–7 (Leipzig: J.C. Hinrichs, 1909), 97–101; Miriam Lichtheim, *Ancient Egyptian Literature: A Book of Readings,* vol. 1, *The Old and Middle Kingdoms* (Berkeley: University of California Press, 1973), 146f.;

B.G. Ockinga, "The Burden of Kha' kheperre' sonbu," *Journal of Egyptian Archaeology* 69 (1983): 88–95.

8 The term corresponds more or less to what Havelock calls "craft literacy": Eric Havelock, *A Preface to Plato* (Cambridge, MA: Harvard University Press, 1963).

9 See Aleida Assmann, *Cultural Memory and Western Civilization: Functions, Media, Archives* (New York: Cambridge University Press, 2011); Jan Assmann, *Cultural Memory and Early Civilization: Writing, Remembrance, and Political Imagination* (New York: Cambridge University Press, 2011).

10 English translations of all of the texts mentioned are to be found in Lichtheim, *Ancient Egyptian Literature*, vol. 1.

11 See Dieter Kuhn and Helga Stahl, eds., *Die Gegenwart des Altertums: Formen und Funktionen des Altertumsbezugs in den Hochkulturen der Alten Welt* (Heidelberg: Edition Forum, 2001).

12 Miriam Lichtheim, *Ancient Egyptian Literature*, vol. 2, *The New Kingdom*, Pap. Chester Beatty IV rto. 2.5–3.11 (Berkeley: University of California Press, 1976), 176f.

13 Herodotus, *Historiae* II ch. 143.

14 Plato, *Timaeus* 22b.

15 See Aleida Assmann and Jan Assmann, eds., *Kanon und Zensur* (Munich: W. Fink, 1987).

16 Paul Zumthor, *Introduction à la poésie orale* (Paris: Éditions du Seuil, 1983), 245–61; see also Aleida Assmann, "Schriftliche Folklore: Zur Entstehung und Funktion eines Überlieferungstyps," in *Schrift und Gedächtnis: Beiträge zur Archäologie der literarischen Kommunikation*, edited by Aleida Assmann, Jan Assmann, and Christof Hardmeier (Munich: W. Fink, 1983), 175–93.

17 A. Leo Oppenheim, *Ancient Mesopotamia: Portrait of a Dead Civilization* (Chicago: University of Chicago Press, 1968).

18 Cf. Assmann and Assmann, *Kanon und Zensur*.

19 Michael Fishbane, *Biblical Interpretation in Ancient Israel* (Oxford, U.K.: Oxford University Press, 1986).

20 Cf. Jan Assmann and Burkhard Gladigow, eds., *Text und Kommentar* (Munich: W. Fink, 1995).

21 Cf. Ernst A. Schmidt, "Historische Typologie der Orientierungsfunktionen von Kanon in der griechischen und römischen Literatur," in Assmann and Assmann, *Kanon und Zensur*, 246–58.

22 Flavius Josephus, *Contra Apionem*, ch. 22, in *The Divine Legation of Moses*, translated by W. Warburton (London: J. and P. Knapton, 1738–41), I, 192f.

23 For this distinction see Jan Assmann, *Das kulturelle Gedächtnis: Schrift, Erinnerung und politische Identität in frühen Hochkulturen* (Munich: C.H. Beck, 1992), 87–103; translated as *Cultural Memory and Early Civilization*, 70–86.

24 Schwartz, "The Age of Transcendence," in *Wisdom, Revelation, and Doubt*, 1–7.

Notes to Chapter 6

1 William Warburton, *The Divine Legation of Moses Demonstrated on the Principles of a Religious Deist, from the Omission of the Doctrine of a Future State of Reward and Punishment in the Jewish Dispensation*, Book 2 (London: 1738–41). Translated by Johann Christian Schmidt as *Dr. William Warburton's "Göttliche Sendung Mosis,"* 3 vols. (Frankfurt and Leipzig: 1751–53).

2 Christoph Meiners, *Über die Mysterien der Alten, besonders die Eleusinischen Geheimnisse* (Göttingen: 1776).

3 See especially Linda Simonis, *Die Kunst des Geheimen: Esoterische Kommunikation und ästhetische Darstellung im 18. Jahrhundert* (Heidelberg: Winter, 2002).

4 See Jan Assmann, *Religio Duplex: Ägyptische Mysterien und europäische Aufklärung* (Berlin: Verlag der Weltreligionen, 2010).

5 Alexander Ross, *Pansebeia, or, a View of all the Religions of the World* (London: 1652).

6 Cited in Winfried Schröder, *Ursprünge des Atheismus: Untersuchungen zur Metaphysik- und Religionskritik des 17. und 18. Jahrhunderts* (Stuttgart–Bad Cannstatt: Frommann-Holzboog, 1998), 228, who refers to the sixth edition, London, 1696, p. 362.

7 Pierre Marestaing, *Les écritures égyptiennes et l'antiquité classique* (Paris: P. Geuthner, 1913).

8 Liselotte Dieckmann, *Hieroglyphics: The History of a Literary Symbol* (St. Louis: Washington University Press, 1970).

9 Diodorus Siculus, *Bibliotheca historia*, III.3,4.

10 Porphyry, *De vita Pythagorae* §§ 11 f., edited and translated by É. des Places as *Vie de Pythagore; Lettre à Marcella* (Paris: Les Belles-lettres, 1982).

11 *Horapollinis Nilotici Hieroglyphica Libri II*, edited by F. Sbordone (Naples: L'Offredo, 1940; translated by George Boas as *The Hieroglyphics of Horapollo* (Princeton: Princeton University Press, 1993); see also Horapollo, *I Geroglifici*, translated by Mario Andrea Regni and Elena Zanco (Milan: Biblioteca universale Rizzoli, 1996); *Des Niloten Horapollon Hieroglyphenbuch*, vol. 1, translated by Heinz Josef Thissen (Leipzig and Munich: K.G. Saur, 2001).

12 Brian P. Copenhaver, *Hermetica: The Greek* Corpus Hermeticum *and the Latin* Asclepius *in a New English Translation* (Cambridge, UK: Cambridge University Press, 1992); *Corpus Hermeticum*, edited by A.D. Nock and translated by André-Jean Festugière, 4 vols. (Paris: Les Belles-lettres, 1945–54).

13 Giordano Bruno, *De Magia* (*Opera Latina* 3, 411–12), cited in Frances Yates, *Giordano Bruno* (Chicago: Chicago University Press, 1964), 263. The connection between hieroglyphics and magic is provided by the church historian Rufinus, who reports that the temple at Canopus has been destroyed by the Christians because there existed a school of magic arts under the pretext of teaching the "sacerdotal" characters of the Egyptians (*"ubi praetextu sacerdotalium litterarum (ita etenim appellant antiquas Aegyptiorum litteras) magicae artis erat paene publica schola"*: Rufinus, *Hist.eccles.* 11, 26).

14 Christoph Riedweg, *Jüdisch-hellenistische Imitation eines orphischen Hieros Logos* (Tübingen: G. Narr Verlag, 1993), 27.

15 John Gwyn Griffiths, ed., *Apuleius of Madauros: The Isis-Book* (Etudes préliminaires aux religions orientales 39. Leiden: Brill, 1975).

16 Jean Abbé Terrasson, *Séthos: Histoire ou vie, tirée des monuments anecdotes de l'ancienne Égypte; traduit d'un manuscrit grec* (Paris: 1731). The book enjoyed enormous success, has been reprinted many times, and has been translated into various languages.

17 "Der, welcher wandert diese Straße voll Beschwerden,
Wird rein durch Feuer, Wasser, Luft und Erden;
Wenn er des Todes Schrecken überwinden kann,
Schwingt er sich aus der Erde himmelan!
Erleuchtet wird er dann imstande sein,
Sich den Mysterien der Isis ganz zu weihn."
(*The Magic Flute*, act II, scene 28). The text is taken from Matthias Claudius, *Geschichte des egyptischen Königs Sethos* (Breslau: G. Löwe, 1777), 155.

18 *Athenian Letters: or, the Epistolary Correspondence of an Agent of the King of Persia, Residing at Athens during the Peloponnesian War. Containing the History of the Times, in Dispatches to the Ministers of State at the Persian Court. Besides Letters on Various Subjects between Him and His Friends*, 4 vols. (London: James Bettenham, 1741–43), vol. 1, 95–100.

19 Ignaz von Born, "Ueber die Mysterien der Aegyptier," 1 (1784): 15–132; Karl Joseph Michaeler, "Ueber Analogie zwischen dem Christenthume der erstern Zeiten und der Freymaurerey," 2 (1784): 5–63; [Joseph Anton von Bianchi], "Ueber die Magie der alten Perser und die mithrischen Geheimnisse," 3 (1784): 5–96; Ignaz von Born, "Ueber die Mysterien der

Indier," 4 (1784): 5–54; Anton Kreil, "Geschichte des pythagoräischen Bundes," 5 (1785): 3–28; Karl Haidinger, "Ueber die Magie," 5 (1785): 29–56; Anton Kreil, "Geschichte der Neuplatoniker," 6 (1785): 5–51; Carl Leonhard Reinhold, "Ueber die kabirischen Mysterien," 7 (1785): 5–48; [Anton Kreil], "Ueber die wissenschaftliche Maurerey," 7 (1785): 49–78; Carl Leonhard Reinhold, "Ueber die Mysterien der alten Hebräer," 9 (1786): 5–79; Augustin Veit von Schittlersberg, "Ueber den Einfluß der Mysterien der Alten auf den Flor der Nationen," 9 (1786): 80–116; Anton Kreil, "Ueber die eleusinischen Mysterien," 10 (1786): 5–42; Carl Leonhard Reinhold, "Ueber die größern Mysterien der Hebräer," 11 (1786): 5–98; Michael Durdon, "Ueber die Mysterien der Etrusker, insonderheit ueber die Geheimnisse des Bachus," 12 (1787): 5–164. See Assmann, *Religio Duplex*, 243–350.

20 [Kreil], *Ueber die wissenschaftliche Maurerey*.

21 See Jan Assmann, *Die Zauberflöte: Oper und Mysterium* (Munich: C. Hanser, 2005), 100–106.

22 Plutarch, fragment 178; see Francis H. Sandback, ed., *Plutarch's Moralia*, vol. 15: *Fragments* (Cambridge, MA: Harvard University Press, 1969).

23 Carl Leonhard Reinhold, *Die hebräischen Mysterien, oder die älteste religiöse Freymaurerey* (1787), edited by Jan Assmann, 2nd ed. (Neckargemünd: Mnemosyne, 2006).

24 Friedrich Schiller, "Die Sendung Moses," in *Werke und Briefe*, edited by Otto Dann, vol. 6: *Historische Schriften und Erzählungen* (Frankfurt am Main: DKV 2000), 451–74.

25 Erhart Graefe, "Beethoven und die ägyptische Weisheit," *Göttinger Miszellen* 2 (1972): 19–21. Beethoven knew Schiller's essay "Die Sendung Moses"; in one of Beethoven's conversation books from 1825 there is an entry by Matthias Artaria: "Have you read 'Ueber die Sendung Moses' by Schiller?" See Maynard Solomon, *Beethoven Essays* (Cambridge, MA: Harvard University Press, 1988), 347 n. 24.

26 Pierre Hadot, *Le voile d'Isis: Essai sur l'histoire de l'idée de nature* (Paris: Gallimard, 2004).

27 "Εγω ειμι παν το γεγονος και ον και εσομενον," Plutarch, *De Iside et Osiride*, ch. 9 (354C) 9–10; see John Gwyn Griffiths, *Plutarch's De Iside et Osiride* ([Cardiff:] University of Wales Press, 1970), 130f., 283f.

28 Von Born, "Über die Mysterien der Aegyptier," 22, translated by Jan Assmann. He quotes Plutarch as his source.

29 Immanuel Kant, *Kritik der ästhetischen Urteilskraft*, in *Werke in 10 Bänden*, edited by Wilhelm Weischedel, vol. 8 (Darmstadt: Wissenschaftliche Buchgesellschaft, 1968), 417.

30   See Jan Assmann, *L'Egypte ancienne, entre mémoire et science*, translated by Laure Bernardi (Paris: Musée du Louvre éditions Hazan, 2009), figs. 1 and 2.

Notes to Chapter 7

1   Jan Assmann, *Moses the Egyptian: The Memory of Egypt in Western Monotheism* (Cambridge, MA: Harvard University Press, 1997); Assmann, *The Price of Monotheism*, translated by Robert Savage (Stanford, CA: Stanford University Press, 2009); Assmann, *Of God and Gods: Egypt, Israel, and the Rise of Monotheism* (Madison: University of Wisconsin Press, 2008).

2   Carl Schmitt, *Der Begriff des Politischen* (Berlin: Duncker and Humblot, 1979).

3   The sociologist Niklas Luhmann says with regard to these differentiations or distinctions of *Leitunterscheidungen*: "Ein Code ist eine Leitunterscheidung, mit der ein System sich selbst und sein eigenes Weltverhältnis identifiziert" ("A code is a leading distinction, by means of which a system identifies itself and its relation to the world") (*Die Religion der Gesellschaft* [Frankfurt: Suhrkamp, 2000], 65).

4   Schmitt, *Der Begriff des Politischen*, 79–95; translated by Jan Assmann.

5   Schmitt, *Der Begriff des Politischen*, 38–39; translated by Jan Assmann.

6   Schmitt, *Der Begriff des Politischen*, 45; translated by Jan Assmann.

7   Ralf Miggelbrink, *Der zornige Gott: Die Bedeutung einer anstössigen biblischen Tradition* (Darmstadt: Wissenschaftliche Buchgesellschaft, 2002); Johannes Fichtner, "Der Zorn Gottes im Alten Testament," *Theologisches Wörterbuch Neues Testament* 5 (1954): 395–410.

8   Cf. Eckart Otto, *Das Deuteronomium: Politische Theologie und Rechtsreform in Juda und Assyrien* (Berlin: de Gruyter, 1999); Hans Ulrich Steymans, *Deuteronomium 28 und die adê zur Thronfolgeregelung Asarhaddons: Segen und Fluch im Alten Orient und in Israel* (Fribourg, Switzerland and Göttingen: Universitätsverlag, 1995).

9   We may even narrow down the time of the composition of Deuteronomy to the time period between 672, the date of the loyalty oaths of Esarhaddon, and 612, the end of the Assyrian Empire. See Eckart Otto, *Das Gesetz des Mose* (Darmstadt: Wissenschaftliche Buchgesellschaft, 2007), 119.

10 See Gabriela Signori, ed., *Dying for the Faith, Killing for the Faith: Old Testament Faith Warriors (1 and 2 Maccabees) in Historical Perspective* (Leiden and Boston: Brill, 2012); Martin Hengel, *Judentum und Hellenismus: Studien zu ihrer Begegnung unter besonderer Berücksichtigung der Situation Palästinas bis zur Mitte des 2. Jh. v. Chr.*, 3rd ed. (Tübingen: Mohr Siebeck, 1988), 464–564.

11 The authenticity of this decree is, however, highly contestable. See Steven Weitzman, "Plotting Antiochus's Persecution," *Journal of Biblical Literature* 123, no. 2 (2004): 219–34.

12 Verses 12–18 in the Authorized Version.

13 For the Jewish concept of martyrdom see Verena Lenzen, *Jüdisches Leben und Sterben im Namen Gottes: Studien über die Heiligung des göttlichen Namens (Kiddusch HaSchem)* (Munich: Piper, 1995).

14 See Aharon Agus, *The Binding of Isaac and Messiah: Law, Martyrdom, and Deliverance in Early Rabbinic Religiosity* (Albany: State University of New York Press, 1988).

15 Mohammad Hassan Khalil, ed., *Between Heaven and Hell: Islam, Salvation, and the Fate of Others* (Oxford and New York: Oxford University Press, 2013). I owe this reference to Dorothea Weltecke.

16 See Jan Assmann, *Religio Duplex: Ägyptische Mysterien und europäische Aufklärung* (Berlin: Verlag der Weltreligionen, 2010), 165–96.

17 For his controversy with J.M. Goeze see Ernst-Peter Wieckenberg, *Johan Melchior Goeze* (Hamburg: Ellert & Richter, 2007), as well as Assmann, *Religio Duplex*, 169–72.

18 Moses Mendelssohn, *Schriften über Religion und Aufklärung*, edited by Martina Thom (Darmstadt: Wissenschaftliche Buchgesellschaft, 1989), 407 f.; this and all subsequent Mendelssohn citations translated by Jan Assmann.

19 Mendelssohn, *Schriften über Religion und Aufklärung*, 420.

20 Mendelssohn, *Schriften über Religion und Aufklärung*, 411.

21 Mendelssohn, *Schriften über Religion und Aufklärung*, 415.

22 Schmitt, *Der Begriff des Politischen*, 55.

23 Schmitt, *Der Begriff des Politischen*, 54–55. The new concepts of human rights and of "crimes against humanity" that were developed after the Second World War prove Schmitt to be wrong. "Humanity" in this sense has no need of enemies.

24 In a note written in the margin of Oskar Goldberg, *Die Wirklichkeit der Hebräer* (Berlin: David, 1925), 49.

INDEX

double membership 128
double philosophy 100, 112
dual society 105

economy 4, 31, 83–84, 115–16, 125,
  128
Eisenstadt, Shmuel 86, 89, 94
election 49; see also Chosen People
Eleusinian mysteries 102, 105
Elijah 51
elite 50, 91, 109, 120
Eloquent Peasant 85
emanation 10, 17, 67
embalmment 10, 21
Engels, Friedrich 46
Enlightenment 4, 25, 42, 95, 127
Epopteia 106, 111
Ernstfall 113–26
Esarhaddon 33–34, 119
Eucharist 48
Eudoxus 105
evolution 2, 19, 43–58, 79–83, 86, 94
evolution of ideas 19, 52, 56–58
exegesis 3, 89–93
Exodus 25–42, 45, 51, 63, 67–68,
  70–77
Ezra 91

faith 38, 47, 68, 124, 126–27
Fénelon, François de Salignac de la
  Mothe 96
Ferguson, Adam 46
Ficino, Marsilio 100, 110
fidelity 49, 119
Fishbane, Michael 90
Flavius Josephus 71–72, 75, 91–92,
  120–21
Fontenelle, Bernard de 97
Freemasonry 104–105, 110, 129
Freud, Sigmund 3, 45, 47, 63–67, 71
friend and foe 4, 113–17, 120, 122,
  126, 128–29
Füssli (Fuseli), Heinrich 110

Geertz, Clifford 84
Genesis 28, 52
Gilgamesh 84, 89
globalization 124, 129
Goethe, Johann Wolfgang 95, 110
Goffman, Erving 38
Golden Calf 29, 76, 117
Gomorrah 117
grammatology 97–99, 101
Greece 3, 26, 33, 81, 83, 85, 88
Greeks 74, 87, 99, 105

Hadot, Pierre 110
Haggai 27–28
Handel, George Frideric 32, 40
Hapy 12, 55
Havelock, Eric 80
Hecataeus of Miletus 87
Hegel, Georg Wilhelm Friedrich
  46
Heidegger, Martin 114
Heliodorus 100
Heliopolis 12, 72, 75
Hellenism 120
Hen kai pan, 100
henotheism 12–13
hermeneutics 90
Hermes Trismegistus 100, 103
Hermeticism 18, 100
Herodotus 87, 99
hieroglyphs 81, 98–101, 105, 111
historia sacra 45
history, written 87
Hittites 121
holocaust 70
Homer 80, 85, 93
Horace 86
Horapollo 100, 111
Horemheb 73
Horus 20, 71, 74
Hosea 27, 28
hurbân 70
Hyksos 26, 53, 67, 70–74, 76